PRAISE FOR
THE LIFE YOU'RE
MEANT TO LEAD

"Tom Hammel is a living example of what it means to win in spite of hang-ups and a scarred past. Tom is well beyond his years in wisdom and practical application of what he has learned and experienced. His new book The Life You're Meant to Lead is a handbook to overcome the past and grasp one's success. I was fascinated by the book as Tom shares his life experience and how we all can aspire to succeed beyond our problems and failures."

Jeff Swaim

Senior Director – Church Relations, Convoy of Hope

"The Life You're Meant to Lead is the perfect picture of a real life story that went from hopeless to hope-filled. I'm forever thankful to be connected enough to watch as Tom's life unfolds into an unstoppable force of good. Tom unpacks his real life experiences and turns them into tools for our use. This is a must read."

Doug Reid

Senior Pastor, Coast City Church

"Tom draws on a wealth of his own life experiences in tracing the solid guidelines for a life full of purpose. His chapter on the benefits of "failure" alone is worthy of an investment in reading this book."

Steve Haas

Catalyst and Influncer

"I love learning from leaders who themselves keep learning and growing! The life trajectory of Tom Hammel powerfully exemplifies this very thing. Tom has a fire in him to excel, but not only for himself; he's on a mission to take as many people as he can with him. This book will spark a fresh fire in you!"

Wendell Vinson
Senior Pastor, Canyon Hills Church

"Tom Hammel is quickly becoming a voice to be heard. His newest book The Life You're Meant to Lead is both profound and insightful. I highly recommend this book to anyone who desires what is possible for their life."

Chris Sonksen
Founder, The Reimagine Group

"My friend Tom Hammel has not only learned the art challenging other people, but the keys to helping them get their life on track."

Gary Garcia
Senior Pastor, Cornerstone Church – Fountain Valley

"The Life You're Meant to Lead is one of the most well-thought-out books I've read. It gets straight to the point, while still showing the vulnerability of the author's life and journey. Tom's message to the reader is that this one life we get is worth LEADING and LIVING!"

Doug Wood
Bestselling author and podcaster

THE LIFE YOU'RE
MEANT TO

LEAD

THE LIFE YOU'RE
MEANT TO

LEAD

10 STEPS TO CULTIVATE PURPOSE
AND AWAKEN GREATNESS

TOM HAMMEL

TABLE OF CONTENTS

FOREWORD

Have you ever wondered:

- *Am I here by chance?*

- *Is there an ultimate purpose for my life?*

- *Am I really the failure I think I am?*

If you have, you've picked up the right book.

It has been said about the Psalmist David that he *"served God's purpose in his own generation."* I've been a ministry leader for 42 years and have been serving my generation—but now, there are new leaders who are serving theirs. Tom Hammel is one of those leaders.

In Tom's debut book, *The Life You're Meant to Lead*, he takes you on a journey through his uncommon life experiences and the powerful lessons learned along the way. Sometimes it's easy to look at a person's success as an adult and think they have always lived a charmed life...but that is not the case for Tom.

From childhood beatings to adolescent drug dealing to contemplating murder, his journey has been anything but "charmed." However, he also found something more: ultimately, the road to redemption and freedom shared in the pages ahead. The book in your hands will challenge and inspire you to never give up on yourself and to always strive for *The Life You're Meant to Lead*.

Rich Guerra
Superintendent, SoCal Network Assemblies of God

PURPOSE
IS PROGRESSIVE

I was seven years old the first time I got high. I discovered my dad's marijuana stash inside a semi-locked box built into the living room coffee table. It was near the cabinet stacked with vinyl records of Pink Floyd and the Eagles. I smoked with a 15-year-old kid who was friends with my sister, but for me, the effect was disappointing. Every evening I had watched my dad get high in the living room, and apparently, my little body had already built up a tolerance.

I didn't do it without getting caught, though. I have three sisters, after all—one seven years older, one five years older, and a twin sister. Nothing got past them, and of course they were going to rat me out. Since I was the only boy, I was usually guilty by gender association in our house.

That summer afternoon, I hightailed it to the pool to escape. I came home in the evening, chlorine soaked and happy. But my dad, who worked long hours and hustled hard to pay for our square, one-story house on Calhoun Way, knew what I had done and confronted me the minute I stepped in the door.

I took a deep breath and waited for him to ream me out. How could I have done something so stupid? I waited for the worst—but it never came.

"I heard you got into my pot," he said sternly. "You don't steal from your old man."

Instead of getting yelled at for doing drugs as a first grader, I got grounded for three days for stealing from my dad. Not what I expected. The punishment didn't stick, and neither did the lesson. A curtain was pulled back that day—not only to the fuzzy pleasure of pot, but the realization that the boundaries around my life were malleable.

I continued to smoke my dad's weed, sneaking to the backyard where we bent and poked aluminum cans into pipes. Drug use wove seamlessly among the mundane—yet ironically steady— home I grew up in. My parents didn't fight. My dad maintained the same job and schedule. We didn't move around. The cops were never at our house. But as kids, we got high and then rode bikes and swam, thinking nothing of it.

My father's pot smoking was routine, normal, shaping my childhood as much as the next memory. Much like a father who comes home, kicks off his shoes and unfolds the newspaper on his lap in the reading chair, it was how my father unwound.

What's "normal" is shaped during childhood by the quiet, consistent influence of the lives around you, and thousands of single memories strung together. Like the grin on my sister's face when we plunked our first fish into the fish tank; the rumble of my father's voice when he called us to the dinner table, religiously, every night; or the smell of burgers grilling in the backyard. In some ways, we were like everyone else.

Your family sets the expectations and the initial trajectory of your life, and while much of my home life ran parallel to other kids in the neighborhood, it took years for me to realize things were different for me.

LIFE-GIVING

Several years ago, my mom dug out my report cards from elementary school and I thumbed through the pages, my mind wandering through the grades and teacher's notes like a person who had started to lose their memory and needed to pick through pieces of their childhood to stitch it all together.

There was an early refrain from my teachers.

"Tommy is a natural-born leader."

"People follow Tommy."

"Tommy influences others."

They applauded my leadership capabilities, but always followed it up with concern that my heart wasn't in the right place. I was "not living up to my potential." I was "distracted rather than helpful." And maybe at the time I was exactly that—distracted, numb, angry, just wanting to get to school and have fun, and slip free of the weight I carried.

I didn't have any guardrails as a kid, at least not parental, anyway. I didn't bump up against boundaries—the kind that gently pushes kids back in the right lane. I clamored for attention in class, purposely challenging any rule or law put in my way; pushing just hard enough to see how flexible it really was. *I had the talent for leadership but not a purposeful intent for it.* It wasn't life-giving, it was life-stealing.

I continued to get high, though the novelty of it had long worn off. The milestones of growing up—like that sweaty-palm, adrenaline rush during your first kiss and the way your heart pounds the first time you drive—disappeared when I did drugs. The drugs muted the thrills.

My innocence, that fresh baby-faced blank slate, that beautiful yet-to-be-spoiled canvas, was stolen from me bit by bit, in ways and situations that I had a hard time reconciling even as an adult. I knew about the mechanics of sex before I even really understood what sex was. My parents' stance on all things racy was this: *you're going to learn it some time, why not now?* And that meant, with a shrug or the turning of a blind eye, I frequently watched raunchy '80s movies, and rattled off sexual jokes like a middle-aged construction worker. It was part of our family's vernacular.

There are helicopter parents—hovering above every rainstorm with an umbrella so not even a raindrop touches their kid. My parents were sink or swim parents. Jump in and get wet. The world is a dirty, complicated place and they felt no need to shelter me from the storm.

I got soaked.

DON'T WASTE YOUR PAIN

Even in the messiness and hurt of my story, I've learned something profound: Our pain is never wasted. It may sound like a sappy greeting card, like something you slide into the basket at a funeral. Telling people, especially those who have experienced incredibly deep wounds in life, that something good can come from their pain seems trite. It seems unfair. But it's true.

I know this well. My pain has been a beacon of strength—a constant, foundational drive for how I live. I'll share more of my story in this book, but what I hope will sink in are not the gory details from my past, but a deep understanding that discovering your purpose is one the most important endeavors of your life. More importantly, it doesn't happen in an instant. The discovery of your purpose is progressive, and that's why it's a lifelong pursuit. There's incredible freedom in that.

THE DISCOVERY OF YOUR PURPOSE IS PROGRESSIVE, AND THAT'S WHY IT'S A LIFELONG PURSUIT."

I've traveled the world, woven a career across five continents, connected with thousands of people, and this has never been more clear to me. Here's what I *know* about you: There is a reason you're here, and nothing about your past disqualifies you from having meaning, purpose, and value.

Pain in life has an uncanny ability of unlocking new purpose. I'm opening my story to you—the beautiful, the wounds, the ugly ups and downs, all of it—because it paved the road to my purpose. I believe your story—with ups and downs of its own—is doing the same if you will let it.

I have used my past and pain in an intentional and purpose-filled way, and in doing so, have done my best to arm people with the tools to find the life they're meant to lead. In fact, I'll be sharing other people's stories throughout this book to shed light on how these tools worked for them. It's been almost twenty-five years since things changed for me and I know without a doubt that if I hadn't been able to see the value in myself, I wouldn't be able to see it in others.

PURPOSE GIVES CLUES

People can give you clues to your purpose, but no one else can tell you what it is. You have to find it, discover it, and hear it for yourself. And then when you find it, you chase it like it's the only game in the world. If you don't know your purpose, have you taken the risks to discover it? Usually, purpose is on the other side of action.

Once you find it and latch on, it is amazingly obvious. It's kind of like riding a bike. It seems impossible at first, but once you get it, you never forget. Finding your purpose seems complicated at certain stages of life, but when you're awakened to it, purpose ignites passion, focus, and motivation. It can't be manufactured because it's independent of all exterior forces, like what others think of you or expect—whether parents, friends, or culture.

When you discover your purpose, the life you're meant to lead suddenly pops into view. It's the path you never even saw the trailhead sign for—a whole new mountain range you get to spend your life exploring. And then you get to go on a great adventure.

In my late teens and early twenties, I didn't yet feel smart or experienced enough to say it at the time, but I learned that my purpose is to guide people to unlock and discover theirs. I went on a journey of trial and error, and my purpose evolved and grew. Out of the gate, I was focused on myself. However, it progressively evolved and I understood it was about much more than me—it was about impacting others. Purposes are funny that way. Rather than being fixed, they change and grow. Your purpose might progress too, and sometimes its growth starts with someone else pointing it out.

From the time I was fifteen, others saw the potential in me long before I did. If you are operating in your passion and purpose,

I TEND TO BELIEVE YOU NEVER ARRIVE; YOU SIMPLY PURSUE."

others will recognize it. It's been true across my journey. I work at it with passion and intensity until I'm called to something else. I tend to believe you never arrive; you simply pursue.

We get scared when we are called to a place where we feel inadequate. We're tempted to say, "Nope! I'm not going to pursue that..." Because purpose puts forks in the road, requiring us to get new tools, resources, knowledge, and education to navigate that road. It means investing time and resources to do something we don't always feel adequate for.

While it's a continual process, the moment you stop being awakened to a fresh direction, you stop growing. And that's when you really stop living, even though you may not be dead. Yes, change can be hard. But it's exciting when we view it as the first pages of a new chapter. What if you were the Indiana Jones of your life, the archaeologist—digging, exploring, and embodying a heart and attitude of possibility? What is behind the next door?

PURPOSE IS CONTAGIOUS

People who awaken to their purpose share it, spread it, grab others by the hand, and lead them in the same direction. It's contagious. It happened to me. I encountered people who were 100 percent sold-out in their purpose, and it helped me realize that I wasn't! So, I made a change and pressed in.

We weren't created to just get by, to just get to the next day until we die. With a small shift of perspective, we could be living life to the fullest. If you were driving on a straight path and turned the steering wheel even a couple centimeters, you'd end up in a completely different state than you first planned. If we move the wheel each day, just a little bit, we can change our world. I wonder, how much joy do we miss each day? I'm passionate about helping people change because so many people I've met live below their possibilities. I know, because I was one of them.

If you don't have a real direction, real purpose, or you're questioning your value, try this: Reflect on what has happened in your past, and instead of letting failures or hurts define and limit you, let them propel you forward.

- What if your pain could be turned into others' gain?

- In what ways could both your wounds and your victories help others?

- How can they help you?

Your past is fixed, right? It's over and done. What is *not fixed* are the Five Ps, your: passion, perspective, platform, process, and of course, purpose. If that sets a flock of butterflies loose in your stomach, that's good. It should! Discomfort is the admission price for growth.

We've all had experiences with people who clearly do not want to be where they are... Like the barista at the coffee shop slamming

DISCOMFORT IS THE ADMISSION PRICE FOR GROWTH."

down my drink while avoiding eye contact. I don't know what's going on in her life, whether she's in pain or bored, apathetic or angry. I do know she's not operating in joy. How different would she treat people if her perspective shifted? If her job was a means to fulfill her purpose?

Sometimes the stones we have to skip across on our purpose journey are wobbly, slick with moss, and not super fun. But when we zoom out, we are able to realize that the biology class we hate... the second job that's draining the life out of us... the dead-end friend group we're stuck in... are all temporary stops on the path to purpose. They're short stints that prepare us for what's to come. Our job is to reframe our current situations and problems as opportunities rather than obstacles.

Finding your purpose is never about a job position. I have encountered the same miserable spirit in high-level executives as I have in the grumpy barista. If you're not where you're supposed to be, it won't matter your income level. If you are in the right place at the right season, roll up your sleeves and make the most of it.

YOUR PURPOSE CONNECTION

You can also discover your passion by noticing what upsets you the most. My wife Jami can walk into a room and immediately spot when the design is messed up. It annoys her. I can't do that, and frankly, I don't care if the design is messed up. In my opinion, any room without at least one Star Wars poster is a problem.

But she's an interior designer, and that's what makes her a good one. I'm a nerd, so I only get to decorate my office. If what you're doing doesn't upset you, stir something inside you, it probably isn't your purpose.

So, what upsets you when it isn't right? What makes you bristle? What could you go on a rant about right now? Now, in a positive light, what are you good at? What do you notice without even trying that no one else does? What would you spend your days doing even if you had Scrooge McDuck swimming pools of money? And more importantly, what are you so naturally good at that it takes little effort or energy for you to learn or absorb?

Check out the following Purpose Connection graphic, which will help you start organizing these thoughts. The first section to fill in is your *rants*, the things that drain you, upset you, and naturally drive you crazy. On the other side are your *raves*, the things that you're good at, that light you up and fill you with joy—like Jami being amazing at interior design. The link between these is *at least* a starting point for your purpose. And notice I said *your purpose*—not anyone else's expectations for you.

Spend some time on your own Purpose Connection before moving on. The link between what makes you come alive and what makes you upset (and immediately want to fix) can be a surprising experience.

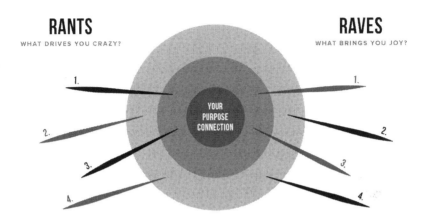

RANTS

WHAT DRIVES YOU CRAZY?

RAVES

WHAT BRINGS YOU JOY?

1.

2.

3.

4.

YOUR
PURPOSE
CONNECTION

1.

2.

3.

4.

IT STARTS IN YOUR HEART

The first time we see our Purpose Connection is exciting. And when I think about it, the first person who comes to mind is actually from my grade school days. Back then, I had to work with a state social worker (because of some tough situations we'll talk about later). This woman handled hundreds of cases over the course of her career. She spent her days working with the most troubled kids. She saw right through my façade and built a relationship with me that no one else could. I let down my guard with her because of the way she treated me. She was fired up about helping kids in bad situations—she was upset by their pain and motivated by her ability to help. It was her purpose.

Any juvenile statistic in our country right now would have put me anywhere but here. Right now, I should be dead, or in jail, or on the street, or in an endless cycle of rehab, or a combination of all of the above. Because of many people like her in my life, fulfilling their purposes to help, I'm not defined by the statistics I *should be*.

You were created with a purpose and a passion, and your life experience becomes a key that unlocks it. Whether that means helping kids in desperate situations or playing music to encourage people in their lowest times or any one of a million other things... It's progressive, and you simply have to open your eyes to recognize it. I found my purpose in the doing.

It starts in your heart. If you're in a miserable job, the way out begins in your heart. Do you need to quit and find something else? Possibly. Until then, decide in your heart to be the kind of employee that makes the company better, to be the employee that sets the example, that others want to be around, that customers respect.

You know you have a change in your heart when your external situation doesn't shift, but your perspective of what happens around you does. You reprogram your brain to find opportunities for your purpose. Your job might not change for now, but you still come every day, not just trying to fill that cup of coffee, not just trying to get that customer through the checkout line or to change that oil. You recognize that while you're doing a task, what you're *really* doing is looking for opportunities to fulfill your true purpose.

When you start thinking like that, there's a new level of expectation to what every day holds.

FAILING YOUR WAY TO SUCCESS

There have been "aha" moments in my life. Moments when I can pinpoint, to the hour, when my life shifted and the trajectory of my future readjusted. But truly, most of my progress in life is much less dramatic. It's been in the small things. In showing up every day, even if I don't feel like it.

I'm going to be honest with you—I feel like I'm going to throw up every time I am about to speak in front of a crowd. Yes, I've been a traveling speaker for almost twenty years—and I should be used to it. I've done it thousands of times. Big crowds. Little crowds. Doesn't matter. I still get scared. But there's nothing else I should be doing right now. All roads have led to this—to share an incredibly important message with people—you matter, you have a purpose, and the world needs you.

Some day, if I'm called away from speaking, it's okay. It doesn't matter where I end up, I have committed to the calling that drives toward my purpose. Behind every encounter with every

FAILURE ISN'T A TIME TO QUIT. IT'S FUEL FOR THE FIRE."

person, I want them to know their value and wake up to the role they have been called to follow.

- What is the fire in your belly?

- What gets you out of bed every morning?

- What has crippled your passions?

I want to empower people to no longer be paralyzed by failure. Failure isn't a time to quit. It's fuel for the fire. It's more pressure on the gas pedal—forward, forward. Every failure in my life served as a bridge to victory, new experiences, and action. Failure should always birth the opportunity to course correct, or try again.

Throughout my journey, I've learned something counterintuitive: Success is found through failure. In the next chapter, I'll share with you how.

FAILURE
LOOPS

Our greatest successes can grow from our worst failures. Abraham Lincoln failed in business, was knocked out by a nervous breakdown, and lost his 1856 vice presidential party nomination. J. K. Rowling was divorced, jobless, penniless, and *nearly* homeless before the first Harry Potter novel was published. Michael Jordan was cut from his high school varsity basketball team. However, one of the brightest minds of all-time helps us see those failures with fresh eyes. Physicist Albert Einstein said, "Success is failure in progress."

When we see incredibly successful people, like those listed above, it's easy to put them on a pedestal. It's alluring to see them like mythological characters who zapped their accomplishments into being. The real story of success is so much more painful, though. The journey to the mountaintop has many valleys. I know this first hand.

By 2005, I had been married to my wife Jami for six years. We were happy. We were in love. We were broke. It was so bad we filed for bankruptcy that year, cataloging an embarrassing (and avoidable) failure. That crappy season taught us a vital lesson: Don't be ruled by debt. While we tripped and fell hard, we got back up, dusted off our butts, and made changes.

Today, we own rental property, have a healthy retirement account, maintain credit scores over 800, and own multiple businesses. Even better, we are more generous than we've ever been. Going through financial failure was the greatest gift because it forced us to get serious about our priorities, our future, and our giving.

Now, I'm not propping us up as successes sharing the stage with Abraham Lincoln, J. K. Rowling, or Michael Jordan... But the hidden secret of failure holds true for everyone—from superstar athlete to a kid like me from Northern California. This means it will work for you too, through a system I created called the Failure Loop.

THE FAILURE LOOP

Do you have negative baggage? Yeah, me too. The truth is we all do. I have failed and you have failed. But that doesn't make us failures. And that's one of the most important lessons. Failure isn't a permanent identity—it's a temporary snapshot in time. It's a tutor along the path. Failure is a better teacher than success. Success is smooth, easy, autopilot, and even deceptive

FAILURE IS A
BETTER TEACHER
THAN SUCCESS."

at times. However, the most dangerous place to be is resting on past success, because it's a good way to lose a desire to learn, blaze trails, and summit mountaintops.

I created a system that demonstrates this perfectly. It's called the Failure Loop, and unfolds in four, repeating phases:

1. **Risk:** trying something new or hard.

2. **Fail:** messing up or missing the mark.

3. **Learn:** reflecting on why and how you failed.

4. **Grow:** applying what you learned as you dust off, and try again.

5. (Repeat)

Visualized, it looks like a continuous loop, with each phase orbiting success.

I think about romantic relationships, particularly that first girl-friend or boyfriend. Attraction is usually what initially draws you together. Maybe you're attracted to the other person's personality or good looks. Maybe your parents are friends, and you ended up spending a lot of time together. But, while promising at first, let's imagine the relationship doesn't last, and painfully crashes and burns. This can feel depressing, isolating, and even embarrassing.

Now, here's where the Failure Loop takes center stage. You have two choices. You can lick your wounds, stay bummed out, and give up on relationships altogether. Or, you can start the learning process. This doesn't mean immediately rebounding into another relationship. Instead, it means reflecting on what went well, what went poorly, and what you have control of doing better next time. Maybe there were some red flags you should've seen earlier, but looked past because you *really* wanted the relationship to work. Or perhaps you made some missteps and weren't the best boyfriend or girlfriend.

Where exactly do you look when you fail? At the person next to you? Down at the floor in shame? Or, do you take a good, hard look in the mirror? What exactly do you need to take personal responsibility for, and what can you release because of the actions of others? There's a difference. If you don't own up to what was yours, you prevent yourself from learning. Crazy, isn't it?

If I have a falling out with a friend, it's a failure in that relation-ship. But how often do I play the victim, refusing to own up to the areas in our friendship where I didn't demonstrate the qualities I expected from them? Honestly, this movement from *failure* to *learning* has a price tag of humility. In this case, my personal challenge is to set aside my pride long enough to ask the tough questions like, *How did I hurt them, even if it doesn't make sense to me? What boundaries did I violate? How did I misunderstand something? Did I communicate well and fairly?*

Relationships are complex, and if I can't embrace where I failed in the relationship, I will be doomed to repeat broken relationships. Like a hamster on a wheel of pain, I'll keep running through the same painful cycles.

It's always less embarrassing to blame someone else. It's hard to admit when we don't have it all together, we drop the ball, we're lazy, we give in to temptation, or we flat out make the wrong decision. But taking ownership of our own failures is the first step to doing better.

BETA TESTING MINDSET

The world is full of opinions, unsolicited or not, and I encourage you to hone in on the voices that come from those you love and respect. When those people give you advice, and you ignore it and mess it up, walk back and acknowledge it. There's a proverb that says, "The way of a fool is right in his own eyes, but a wise man listens to advice." It's a learning process—knowing what is just noise, and what is wise counsel.

Embracing good advice is even part of the business world. Have you ever heard of companies who *beta test* their products? The term *beta* refers to a company sending you a product so they can gather information and ask for advice on bugs, glitches, holes, or anything that's incomplete. It's an admission—we're not perfect, this product is not perfect, and we don't want to fail. So please, help us. We're going to fix whatever is not right, learn, and grow.

When you learn to live in a beta mindset, you're constantly in a position to learn. If you trip and fall on your way to learning what you want out of life—what your true identity is—is it really a failure? Not if you learned something!

Imagine a life without risk. You would never learn to walk, eat, date, teach, or do nearly anything else of value. You would never go outside, because you might get popped in the head by a meteorite. You wouldn't ride your bike, date that girl or guy, drive that car, or take that job. You wouldn't get married. You certainly wouldn't be a parent. Really, you wouldn't live. You have to take the risk, and rebel against the fear. You Risk > Fail > Learn > Grow, and do it again and again.

THE SUCCESSFUL FAILURE

As Jami and I climbed out of bankruptcy, I received a job offer I yearned to take. I couldn't even consider it, though, because we were so underwater financially. My hands were tied and I desperately hated that feeling. It was a defining moment for me, and

I established a new principle in my life to not let finances decide what job I can say yes or no to, or what opportunities I can take. In other words, I decided to live debt free. The question after each failure is this, how are you going to live differently now?

Maybe you need new boundaries, maybe you need to recognize that you are attracted to people who are not healthy for you, maybe you need to see what areas tempt you beyond your control. It will be hard, but don't give up. Set new boundaries, listen and heed the advice of wise counsel, and say no when you need to say no.

Despite the oxymoron, there is such a thing as a successful failure. If you apply a new principle to your life, soften your heart, or kick off a new habit, it's a successful failure. There was more than once in my life, particularly in my teen years, when I stumbled from failure to failure. And now as an adult, I fail and grow, fail and redirect, fail and recalibrate.

Early in my speaking career years, I spoke in Pine Grove, California, where I knew one of the team members there. Onstage that night, I got comfortable and cracked some jokes, many of them at that team member's expense. I had spoken there several times, but the next day I got a call from the leader of the organization.

It seemed, he said, that I didn't like the team member I called on, and like I was out to get him. I was shocked, embarrassed, and hurt that I had come off like a jerk. I blew it. I immediately called and apologized to the person. He forgave me, but I have never been invited back to speak with that organization.

I could have decided right then that speaking and teaching wasn't for me. Instead, I kept on and set a rule for myself: Never try to be funny, especially at someone else's expense. It has made me stronger, more effective, and I don't have to worry about hurting anyone.

If you're operating in your purpose, you're going to fail at some point. It doesn't mean you quit. It means you humble yourself and make changes.

STOP AVOIDING CONFLICT

Life is relational—almost all of it means rubbing elbows with the people around you. Conflict is awkward and uncomfortable, and it's necessary. I'm sure the organization's leader in Pine Grove dreaded picking up the phone to call me out, but I am so grateful he did.

If you tiptoe through life, slinking around every possible conflict because you're afraid, it might be time to add some steel to your spine. It can feel scary, but think of it like this. Avoiding conflict steals your ability to strengthen relationships. Directly addressing conflict is like picking up weights in the gym. You do so carefully, purposefully, and you do it because you want to get stronger. It hurts a little bit, and you're sore the next day,

AVOIDING CONFLICT

STEALS YOUR ABILITY

TO STRENGTHEN

RELATIONSHIPS."

but your muscles get stronger with every repetition. Your relationships can handle a little wear and tear—in fact, just like your muscles, they need it.

It also teaches your heart and mind a valuable lesson: Yes, you can do hard things! You can speak up for yourself, you can love someone who isn't perfect, you can be flexible, you can put someone before yourself, you can stand up for others. More importantly, you can withstand (and grow through) conflict.

When you avoid difficult things (or things that you might fail at), you actually rob yourself of the opportunity to learn skills. This also becomes a habit, or a pattern of avoidance that spider-webs into other areas of your life. I know this well, because the issues in my marriage that have taken the longest to iron out have been the ones we avoided the most.

Jami and I were scared to be honest and transparent for a million reasons. Sometimes because of pride, other times out of a desire to protect each other. Ultimately, it feels easier to keep kicking the rock down the road. It stirs and it stews in both of us until it's no longer a small rock, but a boulder on our shoulders, and we're both feeling the weight.

Breakthroughs in my marriage happened when one or both of us decided we didn't want to stay stuck on that long road of avoidance. And you know what? When we finally face whatever issue it is, the conflict is never as bad as I make it out to be in my head.

We work through it, take heed to whatever lesson it's teaching us, and we're better for it.

HUSTLE, CHEAT, STEAL, DEAL

No one has embraced lessons from the Failure Loop better than my friend Tom (better known by his nickname, TK), who graciously agreed to share his story with you. If you met TK today, you'd see a highly successful entrepreneur, a generous philanthropist, and a man of great character. But if you met him in his teens or twenties, you'd have seen a guy hitting rock bottom—hard.

TK was born in the 1950s, an unexpected half of a set of twins. He grew up in the Catholic church and served as an altar boy. But, as a kid, the sacraments of communion held no holy connection for him. He'd slip off his robe in the back of the church, sneak the wine, and snack on the crackers.

He was raised in the hippie movement, and by the time he was fourteen, he rebelled with gusto. His next fifteen years were reminiscent of my teens. PCP and sex, guns and shame. TK was a loner, drawn to the fast lane, addicted to the same hamster wheel I spent so much time on. He was in and out of the military, in and out of drug rehab, in and out of family life—with that same gnawing feeling that something was missing wherever he went.

It got so bad that, as a new father, he would drive into the most dangerous parts of Los Angeles to score drugs with his newborn son tucked in the backseat. He was in an uncontrolled spiral. It wasn't long before he was bankrupt, living on a stranger's couch, divorced and degenerate, an in-and-out father to that little boy in the back seat. His life was turning out to be a hollow cycle of hustle, cheat, steal, and deal.

In 1987, the lessons in a drug rehab program finally stuck. He got sober, finally kicking the drugs. However, after this massive victory, the real pain set in. With a clear mind and emotions no longer numbed by drugs, he was left to agonize over the things he had done. He cried nearly every day the first year of sobriety.

He was clean, but in the middle of a divorce, with two kids involved, and homeless. To get his feet back under him, he returned to one of his first loves—electronics—by building early-model computer chips. It was the first taste of a future career in technology.

The work sent him to the Philippines where he found the same temptations that he worked so hard to cut off back home. By the time he moved back stateside, he was engaged to a woman he had met online, and his family endured another season of heartbreak. TK's twin brother, who also struggled with addiction (and had even stolen TK's identity at one point), disappeared and was eventually found dead, having driven off a cliff. He was forty-five.

TK faced another decision. He had completed phases one and two of another Failure Loop... Would he bury his pain or let his hurts and personal failures be his teachers? This time, he reflected, searched for meaning in something new, and found purpose in something greater than himself. He began to see ways he could serve others and help them heal through his pain. And also to serve people's needs through his talents in business. Like I said, purpose is progressive, and TK proved that true.

Eventually, he partnered with an old friend who had the financial backing to start a company. It was the start of something good. His company is still in operation today; they install robotic arms for companies like Amazon, UPS, and FedEx.

I'll be straight with you... TK's a millionaire now. Something he wouldn't have been able to handle twenty years ago. He's learned a few things since then. He doesn't want more money. He simply wants to spend more time with his grandkids, to serve more at his church, and to help people avoid the mistakes that tripped him up. His early years were filled with broken Failure Loops— but once he put in the work of learning and applying lessons learned, he grew.

ONE DAY AT A TIME

TK's story is not only about redemption, but about the intentionality that we must use after failure. He did two things that helped him recover from failure. He invested in young people through his work with youth, and he worked to restore healthy relationships with his children.

TK didn't have a relationship with his father, and he struggled to care for his own kids after the divorce from their mother. How do you make up for years of failure? You do it one day at a time. He showed up at baseball games. He provided financial support. He made them a priority. He said he was sorry.

I've been so touched by the deep humility he demonstrated in the years since he turned his life around. In fact, I still remember the first time I asked him to come help out in the youth program after his transformation. It was an emphatic no. He wasn't that comfortable with kids, he was at the start of his journey—what could he possibly have to give to junior high kids?

I kept asking, and eventually he agreed to an eight-week provisional term. TK didn't know what it meant to be called, to have a purpose pulling you like a magnet. He just knew in the first week that he was in the right place. He peeled back layer after layer, and it was a cleansing of sorts—painful, hard, necessary. It was the start of true healing.

The hard road was not over for TK. He was diagnosed with prostate cancer, and we have walked that journey of healing with him. He is cancer-free right now, but the doctor says it will likely come back. It's another hill to climb.

TK's story isn't over, and neither is mine. We're at a comma—not the period. It has been the greatest joy watching him crawl, walk, run, and now soar. He thought he was a failure. He thought he messed up too many times to be loved anymore. But now he's

EVEN THE MOST

SUCCESSFUL LIFE

WILL BE CHECK MARKED

WITH FAILURES."

leveraging years of destruction for purpose and meaning, to bring hope to people.

One of the greatest byproducts of failure is setting up guardrails for others so they don't have to hit the same patches of destruction. This is what I love about his story. It's a reminder that life is messy. Even the most *successful* life will be check marked with failures. It's what you do with that failure that will shape your heart, and in turn, your life.

3 GUARDRAILS

Are there people you work overtime to avoid? You might dodge their phone calls. Ignore their texts. Or leave them on "read"? Here's the truth: These are little clues that the relationship isn't working. For some reason, the relationship is either unfulfilling, or its value is one-sided.

If this sounds like some of your relationships, don't worry, you're not alone! The problem, though, is we tend to feel bad about our avoidance strategies. Usually, this is something we don't like about ourselves. We even start to form an identity as the "bad friend." However, I think there's a more nuanced and helpful way to see these relationships—and every other one in our lives.

The truth is, relationships should fill our lives, not drain them. Often, the people we duck like a dodgeball in third-grade gym class (if you were allowed to play it!) have simply crossed something called a boundary.

THE MOST IMPORTANT WORD
IN RELATIONSHIPS

"Boundary" is a big word for building fulfilling relationships. In fact, it may even be *the* word. Boundaries are your guardrails that *protect* who you really are by setting "do not cross" lines—both for you, and the people in your life. They become the straight-forward rules that determine how you will be treated, as well as how you will treat others.

Simply defined: Boundaries are what you will, and will not, tolerate in a relationship. A boundary is a divider between things. So, in the relational world, a boundary separates you from the behaviors that are okay and not okay. And this goes for how you allow people to treat you *and* how you treat others. But boundaries are tricky things too. Especially when it comes to how you relate to all of the different people in your life.

A great starting place is to pinpoint relationships where you've felt the need to pretend—or to fake it. Especially when you want to get inside someone's inner circle. It may have been the popular kid in high school—or the person with lots of money in your circle today. Either way, when we change how we act to please other people, we've broken a boundary with ourselves. While most of us have acted fake around others to either impress or win them over, it's a losing strategy in the long run.

Think about kids and their parents. What kid is totally them-selves right in front of their parents, the same way they are with their friends? While we will show different sides of ourselves to different people, we should notice areas where we hide or suppress what we love or dream about. Before we know it, we become like a driver drifting outside of his or her lane. We start brushing up against the guardrails meant for our protection.

In eighth grade, one of my close friends stole his parents' car. He lost control of the vehicle and rolled off the road, plummeting into a nearby lake. Sadly, he drowned in the overturned car. The road he was driving on did not have any guardrails. If it had, they may have saved his life. In relationships, boundaries are like those life-saving guardrails. We're going to look at how to set healthy ones. And it starts with us.

ARE YOU A CHAMELEON?

Growing up, I got really good at shapeshifting. At pretending to be one way around my family, another way around my school friends, and then still another way around the rougher crowds I fell in with. I went from group to group, place to place, and my language changed, my body changed, my posture changed— from my house to the hood. Just like a chameleon, who seamlessly takes on the color of its surroundings, I could blend into any group as easy as breathing.

Interestingly, I watched my parents do the same thing. They were different at home than they were at my grandparents' house. They played a part, like we had it all together. Maybe that's why it bothers me so much now when people act like something they're not.

Growing up, I saw this trait in my family. In front of certain people, we were supposed to act like we had it all together. We pretended like we weren't majorly dysfunctional. In fact, I remember calling out one of my family members on this once. I reminded this person that we weren't the Brady Bunch and we shouldn't pretend that we were. It made them so furious, they took down all our Christmas decorations and said we kids were ungrateful! Woah. Sometimes, people are not always who they say they are, and there's such intense insecurity in peoples' hearts and minds that pointing it out feels like an attack.

Now, being a chameleon isn't the same thing as relating differently to different groups of people. That's different than being inauthentic to yourself. No two relationships are alike. I obviously have different boundaries with a stranger than I would with a close friend. You're not a different person, it's that you're operating by a different set of standards. It's okay if you're friends with your boss, but there are still boundaries. There's a dynamic there that if ignored will become a problem.

Boundaries are the authentic expression of yourself in the context of a relationship. They say what you will and will not accept in a relationship. I would allow a close friend to interact with me much differently than how my 12-year-old daughter acts around me. I'm not responsible for the growth and maturity of my friend. The boundaries are different and the permission is different. It's not that I am being authentic to one and inauthentic to the other, but the level of love, concern, and responsibility is different.

I'm clearly more invested in my daughter than nearly any other relationship on this planet. I say that unapologetically. There are friends who I have different levels of investment in too, maybe because of time or shared purpose. The key here is to understand that boundaries aren't the same for every relationship.

Now that we're on the same wavelength about how important boundaries are, what should you do with the relationships where boundaries have been broken—or never set to begin with? It's time to put up fresh guardrails.

BOUNDARIES GIVE LIFE

Who do you avoid? Whose phone calls, text messages, e-mails do you not return because you just can't deal with that person right now? Have you set healthy boundaries that have been violated, or have you set no boundaries and need to do it now because you're mentally, physically, and emotionally drained?

Boundaries keep relationships life-giving. And when things are no longer healthy, boundaries give permission for removal— removal of yourself from a situation, or removal of someone from your life temporarily or permanently when they have violated a boundary.

Clear, healthy boundaries empower you to have pivotal conversations. If you made clear boundaries from the get-go, it takes the personal sting out of reinforcing them. Sitting down with someone you have a relationship with to remind them of your boundaries is simply good communication. There's a reward at the end of that; better boundaries equal healthier relationships and better connections.

I like to think of it in terms of guardrails and guide rails. The guardrail keeps you on track and focused in relationships; it keeps you safe and healthy. The guide rail takes it a step further by keeping you in the correct lane so you can get to your destination of purpose.

BOUNDARIES IN KEY RELATIONSHIPS

The number of relationships and their complexities could take up a whole book, so we're going to hone in on the three most common (and significant) ones: parents, romantic partners, and friends. Let's kick it off with dear old mom and dad!

Parental relationships are the greatest example of relationships being evolutionary. While the parent-child relationship is clearly defined, it should constantly grow, change, and adapt with age. There should be a natural growth of boundaries as you mature and grow older, and take on more ownership of your life.

When my daughter turned seventeen, my job was to allow her to take on the responsibilities of a 17-year-old. She didn't need the responsibilities of a 20-year-old, and yet, she didn't need the boundaries or guardrails of a 12-year-old.

A parent who doesn't open up boundaries as their kids get older are not allowing the natural evolution of the relationship. Healthy boundaries do two things that create tension. Boundaries that adjust at the right times create a safe space for kids to learn and grow, while also constructing a "fence" that keeps them from straying too far.

A social experiment conducted years ago studied the effects of having no fence around the playground of preschool children. When there was no fence, the children remained huddled around their teacher. Once the fence was up, the kids roamed, explored, and bumped against the boundary holding them in because they felt safe. As parents, we have to be mature enough to know when to expand the boundaries.

The life you're meant to lead allows for boundaries that grow and expand as you mature. People tend to not set boundaries in their life, or they continue to live by the boundaries their parents set. Fear keeps them from transcending their adolescent boundaries. Even adults in their thirties and forties sometimes still make decisions based on whether their parents would approve. It could be something as small as cutting your long hair, or as significant as buying a house.

As an adult, you've accepted a boundary or limitation of yourself in a way that might not be healthy or life-giving. Living in fear is never a good boundary, especially if you are old enough to respect your parents and still make the best decisions for your life.

Living in a place of fear can also create a victim mentality:

> "My family says…"

> "They won't let me do…"

> "It's their fault that I'm not living the life I want to lead."

It's not a boundary they have created; it's one you have created and decided to live within. You've passed the responsibility on to them. I see people stuck in that space.

HOVER OR HANDS OFF

Growing up with a parent who didn't set boundaries, or growing up with a helicopter parent who constantly hovered, requires you to reset the boundaries in your life as soon as you are able. I say this with much love, but the craziest people on the planet are moms of boys (especially when they're in junior high!). They hover over their babies, protecting, suffocating, creating boundaries that are not really boundaries because their sons never actually have the chance to walk without holding on to their mamas' hands. It's unhealthy.

The boys cannot start to develop their own boundaries with people because Mom is always there. It stunts their social growth because they never have to get out their own tool set to solve problems, assert themselves, or correct a mistake.

When they do get out on their own, it's easy to go off the deep end because they don't know the boundaries without Mom there. All chaos breaks loose in their life and they enter a season of destruction. All children need to learn not to touch the stove—not just because Mom said not to, but because it's hot and they could get burned. You shouldn't run in the street because you could get hit by a car and die. You shouldn't lie because it diminishes your word.

How do you create a safe space to fail without being completely hands off or hovering like a helicopter? We do it in our house by striking a balance. My daughter had a boyfriend recently and instead of getting Dad-macho and forbidding her from seeing him, I invited him into our home. Where else is my daughter going to have safe boundaries to fail at a relationship? I want her to learn healthy boundaries in relationships—both emotional and physical—while under my supervision.

When we refuse our children the opportunity to figure out boundaries, we're simply trying to make ourselves comfortable, because we don't want them to fail. We don't want them to get hurt. But it's not really about us, is it?

On the other end, far away from the helicopter Moms, are the parents who think their kids can learn it all on their own. That was my experience and I took full advantage of it. More than kids getting into things they shouldn't, not setting boundaries communicates a very damaging message: I don't actually care enough about you to set boundaries for you. I don't value your safety, I don't value you. And while that might not be true, it sends a message that says: I don't love you.

If you love someone, you have to tell them no sometimes. Some of the kids who love and respect me the most today are the ones I kicked out of our youth program years ago.

I think of a boy who was in a group I led, who had absolutely no guide rails in life. I was the only person he knew who consistently followed through on what they said. No one had established boundaries for him—not his parents, principal, police officers, or teachers. I set the boundaries, he violated them, and I kicked him out.

I went to his house to meet with him and his parents. I informed them that I called the police and he would not be allowed where the group met for six weeks. If he came, he would be arrested. He was incredulous. How could I do this to him? He felt the unfamiliar confines of a boundary, and he wasn't sure how to react.

IF YOU LOVE SOMEONE,

YOU HAVE TO TELL

THEM NO SOMETIMES."

After six weeks, he came back and we went through the steps to heal and learn. I communicated to him that I cared about him, I valued him, and I didn't want him making decisions that would lead him away from his purpose. He told me I was the only person he knew who set boundaries and actually stuck to them.

WHAT DO YOU WANT?

What if you sat down and crafted the perfect relationship scenario with parents, your significant other, and your friends? What would you give? What would you get? What does a healthy relationship in each of those areas look like?

After you know those important points for each relationship, work backward from that end goal to set the boundaries that would build those ideal relationships.

Anything outside the boundaries becomes toxic to the goal. Sometimes the goal is just to have fun. Sometimes the goal is love, companionship, and intimacy. If you know that from the beginning, you can set the boundaries accordingly. Even more, you can ask yourself, is it practical? Is it reality? Is it healthy to get those things from this relationship? If you're looking for personal worth and ultimate fulfillment in a romantic relationship, you're looking in the wrong place. It's not fair to that person to put that responsibility on them.

Healthy boundaries are for everyone, even for our own thoughts. You set boundaries and work to eliminate thoughts that aren't in line with who you are. Negative self-talk is nothing but destructive. How you speak about yourself—your body, your actions, your desires—all play a part in how you view yourself. Is your head filled with negative, poisonous criticism that will never lead to anything but poor self-worth?

We do so much critiquing, but what is your reward for accomplishments? How do you celebrate the times you have stayed on the path and have found success? Don't wait until the finish line to celebrate. Recognizing each accomplishment will motivate you to keep going.

The bottom line is you cannot set healthy boundaries and guide rails with your parents, your romantic partners, and your friends until you have set healthy boundaries with yourself. If you don't value yourself enough, or think you're worthy enough to set up boundaries within yourself, you won't do it with others.

ROMANTIC

I played with fire years ago, running from girl to girl to girl, looking for the affection I had not received from my parents. I craved attention and love, and I thought I could find it in romance. I was wrong. And by not setting boundaries in that area of my life, I violated all sorts of physical and emotional constraints that would have served me (and my romantic partners) well.

I learned that once those boundaries are broken, it's extremely difficult to stop crossing them. There was a girlfriend I was trying so hard to be honorable with—but because I had destroyed romantic boundaries in every other relationship, I failed time and time again.

This behavior also surfaced insecurity in my relationships, driving me to behaviors that were inauthentic to who I was. It was toxic. I remember a girl standing on my front door, pounding and screaming for me to let her in, and at the time, I was barely in my teens.

It harms you. It harms them. It's a sword that cuts both ways. Violating sexual boundaries will never fulfill whatever it is you're looking for in that person and harm your romantic partner as well. It's fleeting, it's hollow, and it will never provide true satisfaction.

It's like eating a meal, but that feeling of hunger never subsides. The more you eat, the hungrier you feel. Emotions in a relationship with no boundaries are the same. Jealousy, which can be expressed in a healthy way, often springs from insecurity. If you are in a relationship with someone and they want more time with you, that's wonderful *as long as*: it makes you feel more loved, doesn't deter you from your purpose, and isn't controlling.

If jealousy brings out the worst in you, isolates you from others, distracts you from your purpose, and causes you to make poor decisions, it's a red flag. If it's isolating, it is not a healthy relationship because we are all built for community. I've seen romantic relationships isolate people from their parents, from their social groups, from their friends. Honestly, that's how cults work.

There's a lot to be said about healthy boundaries within romantic relationships. The guardrails become love and care. In a healthy relationship, you do certain things out of affection—and never because they are demanded of you. This means you've set a boundary of care, and not control. You may love them, yet still avoid certain situations that can lead to sexual compromise before you're married. This means you've set boundaries on how and when you'll express romantic love.

While you want to communicate and agree upon key guardrails like these, you certainly don't have to be exactly alike. A couple can have different purposes, but it's wonderful to at least have complementary purposes. That allows you to deeply invest in your partner's vision for life because you're headed the same direction. It's unity of vision and value, and you can champion each other's purpose.

Can you imagine being with someone whose purpose you couldn't understand or support? They would spend time, energy, and resources on something that didn't align with your life, and it would drain the life right out of your relationship.

ARE YOU FOR REAL?

It hurts me to think of how many people walk around this planet desperately looking for worthwhile friendships. You know, that deep, genuine, I'm-not-leaving-no-matter-what kind of friendship. It's hard to find, and even harder to maintain. But I truly think it is possible if we act authentically, invest genuinely, and honor boundaries. Real friends with healthy boundaries will support, motivate, and challenge us.

If you did an inventory of your friendships, how many of them exist just to please the crowd? How many are friends who you've gained without any sense of loyalty—who won't call you on your crap? What compromises are you making to keep those friends around? Your morals? Your vocabulary? Your activities? What you eat? What you wear? Anytime you're not behaving authentically, it means you're violating a boundary that should've already been set. We don't flourish in relationships when we aren't authentic.

A friend who is truly invested will know the real you. They will support your purpose, but not rubber-stamp your every whim. They're not a full-time cheerleader, they're a friend. There's a difference. Your closest friends, the ones in that inner circle, will more than likely have a similar vision, even if it's manifested differently. A close circle of friends could be a mix of full-time working moms and stay-at-home moms. They have all chosen different approaches to how their household is run, but they all are working toward the same thing—being a great mom.

WE DON'T FLOURISH

IN RELATIONSHIPS

WHEN WE AREN'T

AUTHENTIC."

While I have a wide variety of friends, my closest ones challenge my motives and behaviors the most because they get to see the real unplugged Tom. If they see something in my life that is out of sync with my character or my purpose, they ask me about it. They have permission to call me on my crap—and I expect them to—because they have my back like nobody else.

I'm not looking for friends to tell me I'm always right. My closest friends cheer me on, but are invested in more than my feelings. They are invested in me as a person and they know the value of balancing encouragement with helping me grow. Clearly we want people who encourage us after we fall, but we also want them to be grounded in a sense of reality and to desire our growth. It's a tricky boundary to navigate, which is why deep, genuine friendships are rare and special.

BOUNDARY BROKEN!

How do you know when you've broken a boundary? You can feel it. There's restlessness, there's pain, your stress levels go up. You'll see red flags when you are habitually violating a boundary in a relationship.

Are you putting in more hours to try to overcompensate for a violation that is taking place? Are you overeating? Are you heading to the gym way too much because you don't want to be at home? Outlets, especially physical outlets, can be good. But not when you're just trying to escape something relational. You can't fix your marriage by running one more mile on the treadmill, eating that extra bag of chips, or yelling at your kids.

If your boundaries keep getting run over and you are trying to take control by overcompensating in another area of your life, you will not have peace. There's no serenity. No wholeness. No anchor. That's how you know a boundary has been broken.

LIVE MULTI-DIMENSIONALLY

We rob ourselves the opportunity to discover new things and grow when we lock ourselves in relationships with people who are only like ourselves. I'm a white, 40-year-old married man with teenagers in the house. If I only hung out with other white, 40-year-old married men with teens, I would have a one-dimensional view. There's no diversity or reality check!

Do you spend time with people who look, think, and believe differently than you? People who come from different places than you? If not, please open yourself to new relationships. That might mean serving on a nonprofit board with a group of strangers, or offering to help that neighbor you only wave to in passing. There are incredible people just a step or two outside your comfort zone.

Diversity in your relationships exposes you to worlds that might look very different from your own. When I think about all the food I've ever eaten, it's awful to think of how plain the menu

WE CAN LEARN FROM

EVERYBODY, BUT ONLY

IF WE'RE GENUINELY

INTERESTED."

would be if I had only spent time with one demographic. I have friends from all over the world, and I can relate to so many different kinds of people because I truly see the value in connecting with people different than me.

The best way to grow my social influence and social circles is not to be interesting, but to be genuinely *interested* in people and their stories, and then ask myself: What can I glean from it? What can I learn? One of my guide rails—the paths to living my purpose—is to learn from everybody. I learn from my teenage daughter all the time. It's so empowering and it honors her. We can learn from everybody, but only if we're genuinely interested.

People get stuck because they only spend time with people who have the same career path, finances, education, or background. Set a goal that includes building healthy relationships with people who are living a life you would like to emulate. Be yourself, be authentic, and create relationships with people who are successful in the areas you desire to grow in. If you want more financial freedom, spend time with people who are already there. Want to be a writer? Hang out with writers. Want to want to be a musician? Hang out with musicians. It doesn't mean that you do it to the exclusion of everyone else. Just approach relationships with a desire to learn, grow, and invest. There is always an area where we can become better. I want to be a better husband, so I want to spend time with men who are doing just that.

On the other side, I've set boundaries that I don't hang out with men who treat their wives like a ball and chain. No one in my close circle makes wife jokes. I've eliminated them from my life because I don't want that kind of influence and thought pattern around me. Whenever we spend time with someone, we are reinforcing, removing, or creating new thought patterns. It's a constant wax and wane. Our brain gets reprogrammed a little each time we converse with someone else. What, and who, are you allowing into your mind?

IT'S ALL ABOUT QUALITY

If there was only one piece of relational wisdom I could share with someone, it would be to set boundaries. You have to have boundaries in every single relationship. I have boundaries even in my marriage, though some would disagree. I believe in marital boundaries like fighting fair and agreeing to have pivotal conversations. There should be guide rails to how you will grow, how you will parent.

My wife and kids know that I love them. They can be secure in that. It's an every-moment, all-day, forever thing. For my kids in particular, it gives them the courage to take risks. They are never going to mess up so badly that I won't love them. My wife and I have created a space for them to fail.

My wife and I call each other out on what needs to be improved, but we have boundaries in the way we speak to each other. She doesn't nag. I don't rule the house. We are teammates.

She doesn't parent alone. I don't parent alone. We established a boundary at the start of our parenting years that disobedience is dealt with immediately. There's no "wait until your father gets home" mentality. Jami disciplines right away if I'm gone. I don't want them to be afraid of me when I come home.

We also set boundaries around corporal punishment with our kids. We never spanked out of anger. It was in an atmosphere of control. I told them how many spankings they were getting, and why. There was a boundary there, because I never wanted to punish out of anger. The endgame of a punishment is not to release anger for the parents, but to bring correction to the child. Here was the boundary. You crossed it. This is the punishment.

And it always ended with love. Once I spanked my children, I held them until they were done crying. I didn't spank them and then leave them all alone. You violated a boundary, you were punished, and I'm going to stay with you until you're okay. I stayed as long as needed, until we talked and they felt secure, and then we could go back to playing or doing whatever it was we were doing.

We spanked with the spoon, and loved with the hand. Anytime I reached for my kids they never flinched because I have never spanked them with my hand. My hands are for embracing, hugging, holding, and affection. My kids still hold my hands to this day. My 17-year-old daughter and I were at the mall last week and she still held my hand for a bit. They know my hands are for love and that is how it will always be.

My kids are huge blessings in my life. My wife and I didn't do it perfectly, but we stayed on a consistent path because we were purposeful in setting boundaries for our kids. It wasn't all about keeping them inside the boundaries, but rather helping them get strong enough under our care, so that someday they could build and maintain their own guide rails.

That's the great thing about boundaries. You're bumping up against them as you move toward something. You can't stay stagnant. And that's what we tell our kids. We're going to challenge you to grow, and we're going to celebrate and champion that growth each time you get to the next marker. We want our kids, and each person we are in a relationship with, to keep moving forward, developing and fulfilling their destiny.

RE-SCHOOLED:
AN EDUCATION IN PEOPLE

Consider the word *education*. What does it bring to mind? School, grades, classes, teachers, papers, college, degrees. I'm game for all of it. A traditional education is valuable. But it should never be the totality of your learning, particularly if you are a leader.

I had the capacity all my life to be an honor student. I was identified as "gifted" early in elementary school, but my rebellion kept me from excelling. I could have skipped grades if I had actually applied myself, but I was more interested in partying. My focus wasn't in the classroom.

What I did learn during those years, though, was how to observe, ask questions, travel, and soak up information from people smarter than me. I survived on the street because I learned about people. I studied their gestures, mannerisms, habits, and motives. And later on, I took those skills, my scrappiness, my perseverance, and those street smarts to earn a master's degree. You can build a path of traditional learning and experiential learning. It's what I call a unicorn education. It's rare, but it will get you places.

If there is one thing to glean from my childhood and adolescence, it is this: Education is deeper and richer when we embrace the learning that happens around us every single day, especially outside of the classroom.

PEOPLE SKILLS

Here's one of the greatest textbooks you can study for absolutely free: people.

At the end of the day, your education really isn't about you. It's about learning to bring value to others. So, become a student of people. Watch them, and discover their strengths. When you learn their strengths, you add value to their life. It's in line with my mission statement—find and discover people's strengths and match that with God's plan for their lives. To truly help people, you have to find out where they excel, where they are naturally gifted, where they naturally lead.

I absolutely think there is value in a college degree, and it's worth much more than a bigger paycheck. Its value is exponentially

AT THE END OF THE DAY,
YOUR EDUCATION REALLY
ISN'T ABOUT YOU.
IT'S ABOUT LEARNING TO
BRING VALUE TO OTHERS."

greater if you have also been educated in people. I am amazed at how many bosses and managers have outstanding credentials on paper, but struggle to lead well. The work culture they create fosters an environment of distrust and discouragement. They earned their degrees, but their value is diminished because they didn't marry it with people skills. A leader who has learned how people work encourages, builds unity, and creates an atmosphere of teamwork.

If you only have one—either a degree or people skills—you're lacking the full compass of your potential. If you're only people smart, that can lead to manipulation. If you're only book smart, you're only useful to a certain segment of society. You're like a doctor who knows all about medicine but doesn't have good bedside manners.

Learning how people work is not about manipulation, but genuinely listening, learning what they need, and then aligning your leadership to draw out the best in them. That's why we ask so many questions, and then we shut up and listen. It's really an art. There's not a school to learn that kind of education. It comes through trial and error.

Master the art of conversation and you will be equipped with the skills, tools, and knowledge to apply what you have learned and to lead well. Become a student of people, match it with your book smarts, and you will gain the ability to help people identify their purpose and live it out.

A LEARNED ART

If you've ever been in a car with a 5-year-old, you know it's a ride packed with nonstop questions... "Dad, what's that green thing?" "Mom, when are we going to eat?" "Dad, why does it smell so funny in here?" Kids are like little journalists. They don't just ask the *why* questions, they want to know who, what, where, and when. And that sponge-like spirit of endless curiosity is what we need as adults. We need to become masterful at asking questions.

I received a phone call from a business leader who was resigning and wanted to pass along a list of people he would recommend to take his place. He was calling to ask if he could add my name to the list. I was honored but immediately had questions. I wondered about the position, about the process, about his experience. In a conversation with him several months later during my third interview for the job, I asked him what made me stand out. His answer was simple—I was built for the job because I was the only one who asked questions first.

That's a pretty simple way to qualify for a promotion, right? But it's telling. Most of the other candidates were smart, driven, and well-equipped to do the work. However, the difference was the art of curiosity.

We have to stop running through life without pausing to ask the questions that will direct us on the best paths. Truly, the first step of education is learning to ask the right questions—sometimes

DON'T JUST COPY
AND PASTE WHAT YOU
LEARN, BUT MOLD IT
TO YOUR PURPOSE."

we're learning what to do, and other times what not to do. Have I learned from my own mistakes? From the mistakes of others? When you're learning from someone else's experiences, it's as if they are paying the tuition for your schooling. You get a full-ride scholarship to the lesson they just learned.

I have made it my mission to learn what to do and not to do from the people around me, and that includes everything, from communication and leadership to relationships and financial decisions. I have saved myself a lot of heartache over the years by gleaning from others. You can learn much just by watching the way other people live their lives. Warren Buffett reads five to six hours a day (and once advised hopeful investors to read 500 pages of corporate reports daily). That's great, but for me that would mean I couldn't run a company anymore.

That's where questioning comes in. Why does billionaire Warren Buffett read six to eight hours a day? What mindset produces those actions? Then you can take that mindset and make it portable. I learned from Buffett that reading every day gives you context, makes you more informed about the world, keeps you on top of current events, and helps you hone in on the areas of your life where you want to grow. Reading is important, and I now read thirty to sixty minutes a day. I took his mindset and applied it in a way that worked best for me, and it's made a difference in my life. Don't just copy and paste what you learn, but mold it to your purpose.

When I was younger, I also learned to study how other people approach problems. When I asked my parents permission and the answer was no, I asked why. Even though they were hands off in some areas, they were strict in others. If they said I couldn't spend the night at a friend's house, I asked for their reasons. It wasn't to argue. I wanted to learn the system. Whatever reasons they gave, I would learn from that, and eliminate those reasons for saying no before I asked again.

It might have been to dance around my parents when I was young, but as an adult, this skill has allowed me to anticipate problems before they come up in a job, work through issues with my kids, and make decisions about my future more efficiently. In the past, when I considered a job, I was the candidate that immediately asked deep questions. I never took a job just to pad my resume. It had to truly be a position that helped me live out my skills.

As a parent, I refuse to say "because I told you so" to my kids. If my answer is no, I have a reason. Yes, they argue their case, and I love it when they ask questions. Understanding the why is not a way to outsmart other people, it's taking the knowledge and applying it to the future.

Make sure you're asking questions of the right people in the fields where you need to grow. If I need to improve my finances, I'm going to ask people who have conquered that area of their life. Not just someone who is wealthy, but someone who is a good steward of the resources they have—I've seen many people who have had a lot of money end up broke.

Wisdom often comes with experience, which often comes with age. Don't be afraid to ask for advice from someone older than you. They've experienced both success and failure. They've walked the road already, so why not ask them where the potholes are? You should be asking people who are older than you for parenting advice, marriage advice, purchasing advice, spiritual advice. Anybody who has more trips around the sun than you will have insight. Don't be too proud to ask.

Then there are the people who always have your best interest at heart. Ask thought-provoking questions and truly listen to the people who love you. It's amazing what happens when you stay curious to understand how their minds work and how they approach problems. A great mentor can act like a software update for your mind—the deeper you listen, the better you get. Outside of mentorship, this is true of real life too.

THE SCHOOL OF REAL LIFE

When I was in graduate school, getting my master's in organizational leadership development, I did all of the typical "school" stuff. I read thick books and wrote papers. (Ah, the joys of school!) However, my final project was an eight-page business plan. If you've never created (or read) a business plan, just think of it like a blueprint for a skyscraper, only it's for, you know, a business. They are in-depth and burn through a lot of brain cells.

During school, I still worked full-time. And when this final project rolled around, I happened to be in charge of a large conference that would have almost 4,000 junior high and high schoolers. This conference has happened every year for decades. But there was a big problem—and my boss asked me to fix it. The event lost money every year. And while its goal wasn't to *make* a big profit, it did need to at least break even to be economically sustainable.

That was my job. So I analyzed the event, looking at every detail of the budget, from expenses to registration fees to everything in between. I found places to save serious money and restructure the conference by methodically walking through the numbers. Then, I turned that data into a plan to help the conference keep itself alive—and keep 4,000 students amped up to do amazing things in the world every year.

Now, besides the joy of helping others, I also got to use this plan for my final project. It had every element of the assigned business plan. Only instead of being theoretical, it was real. It was a blueprint for a large organizational event to function indefinitely.

I don't share this story with you to brag about my nerdy financial skills. Instead, I want you to see that real world experience has *huge* educational value. I do value my formal schooling, as it helped me professionalize my street skills. But, going to re-school by being a constant learner outside of the classroom is the best way to grow and educate yourself in practical ways.

GO BACK TO RE-SCHOOL
AND MAJOR IN QUESTIONS

You see, real life is tricky. It doesn't always have lesson plans and assignments like in school, where every problem has a "right" answer. Sometimes, the issues we face aren't really the issues we think they are. Here's what I mean.

Imagine a friend is confiding in you about their next job opportunity. They ask you for advice, "Should I take the new job, or stay in my current one?"

Jobs are a big deal, and this can be a super stressful decision for people. On the surface, your friend should just weigh the pros and cons, right? They should compare wages, bosses, coworkers, working conditions, hours, and all the other details that make up a working life. However, is the question *really* about which job has the more attractive checklist?

What if, instead of giving your friend an answer based on the job that wins the tally-mark contest, you started with questions like this: *Are you looking because you're trying to escape your current situation? Or because it's in alignment with your next season?*

See the difference? Suddenly, instead of staying surface level, you're plunging into the *real* motivations of making a leap. You're asking questions centered around purpose. You're also serving your friend well. Because if they're trying to escape their current job for greener grass, they're not really going to escape. The new job will have its own problems and drawbacks. Especially if your friend is creating any of the drama or problems themselves. They'll just hop in the backseat and come along for the ride!

THE 30-DAY #RE-SCHOOLEDCHALLENGE

Alright, now I have better than a school assignment for you to continue your learning in re-school. It's a 30-day challenge to ask questions before giving any answers. The next time anyone asks you for advice or your opinion, respond with questions first, seeking to understand what's at the heart of the issue. I predict you'll learn a lot about how people work and how you can add more value in any setting—whether at work or in your personal life. Here's how even simple questions might play out:

> **Your friend:** I want to buy a new car. Which one should I get?
>
> **You:** Why do you want a new car, is something wrong with your current one?
>
> **Your friend:** Nothing's wrong with my car. I just want a new one.
>
> **You:** Okay, good to know. Why?
>
> **Your friend:** I'm embarrassed about how old my current car is.
>
> **You:** Why does that matter? I thought you're trying to save money to pay off your student loans.

Your friend: Well, I want to impress [insert potential significant other].

You: Do you think they're the kind of person who cares about the car you drive?

Your friend: Hmm. Maybe not. I guess I'm not sure.

You: So maybe you don't know them super well. What if you grabbed coffee with them first?

Now, before you roll your eyes at this simple conversation... Let me ask you a question. Do you know the number one emotion people feel when buying a new car? Is it a sense of security? Nope. Is it excitement? Close... but no. According to a study, it's confidence.[1] That's right, the primary emotional driver for picking up a new ride is *confidence*.

For some reason, new cars give people an overwhelming boost of confidence. What other revelations could asking questions unveil? Take the challenge and find out in the next thirty days with the #Re-SchooledChallenge. (Share what you learn on social media and tag me on all social platforms @TomHammel.)

---

[1] Emily Anderson, "The Consumer Car-Buying Journey Is Emotional," Martec, 12 June 2019, www.martecgroup.com/emotional-car-buying-journey/.

MONEY,
MONEY, MONEY

Remember your birthday parties as a kid? When you were really little, you wanted the presents in the biggest possible boxes. To your little mind, the larger the package, the better the gift. Then, you got older—and *way smarter*. You probably started to get more excited about envelopes than boxes and bows. And that's because every envelope screamed: *money, money, money!*

I trusted my parents with my first real chunk of birthday cash. It was a check for my fifth birthday and I gave it to them to take to the bank and cash. I never saw it again. It was the first time I felt a lack of control with finances, and it was at the tender age of five when I realized I wanted to keep track of my own money.

Even at five, I had a pretty good understanding that money is powerful. It would take me years to understand the widely varying ways it can be used—for good, for evil, as an idol, as a tool to help others. Most importantly, my journey with money has taught me there is no way to divorce money from your purpose.

EITHER YOUR MONEY IS
WORKING FOR YOUR PURPOSE,
OR YOUR MONEY IS WORKING
AGAINST YOUR PURPOSE.
THERE'S NO GRAY AREA."

Either your money is working for your purpose, or your money is working against your purpose. There's no gray area.

During elementary school, I worked at my aunt's house during my spare time, cleaning and doing yard work. I saved the money she gave me for a skateboard, and in doing so, developed some self-control by resisting the instant gratification that comes with spending as soon as you get a little money. I eventually convinced my aunt to buy me the skateboard on loan. She held me to it, and I paid her back. Another lesson was born—I didn't like the feeling of being in debt to someone. It was just another way I didn't have control over my own money.

I learned through those first two experiences that I was going to hustle to make my own money. I started collecting soda cans and doing odd jobs to earn cash. With my savings, I bought gum and candy, a $70 baseball bat, a Walkman. My parents didn't have a lot of money, and I learned to save, barter, and trade. I eventually stopped asking for Christmas presents. I just wanted money. I wanted it bad enough to break some rules. By the time I was eleven, the small wad of cash from cleaning and can collecting wasn't enough. I had tasted the fruit of buying power, and I wanted more.

THE STREET PHARMACIST

The people I was around during my early teens showed me a new way to earn money and gain power in my life: selling drugs.

Selling gave me the financial independence from my parents I desperately sought. And it gave me money to buy more drugs.

It was a slow takeover. Like the venom of a snake, the need for money started to pump through my veins. There are numerous neuroscience studies that look at the brain chemicals and the dopamine that are released when you buy something. It's self-medication, and the more you go through the cycle, the more you need to reach the levels to match that first high—a cycle much like what I went through using the drugs I was selling. So your next purchase has to be bigger, riskier.

It doesn't happen overnight. There are red flags along the way. The first is that we buy to escape something or medicate emotional gaps in our lives. The second is that we feel entitled, like we deserve that new car (which we can't afford) because we've never owned one before... Or we've had a rough week, so we've earned those new clothes. And the third red flag is, sometimes, we buy stuff we don't need to impress people we may not even like! We spend to keep up with the Joneses (who are in crippling debt, by the way, but don't tell anyone).

When any one of these three deadly financial motives drive our spending, money controls us, instead of us controlling it. And this behavior can quickly take over our lives without us even knowing it. Remember the saying about the frog and the kettle? This is more like the spender and the credit card. Debt rises, slowly but surely. Dollar by dollar, interest by compounding interest, and we're in deeper than we ever planned.

MONEY IS A RESOURCE AND TOOL; NOT THE ENTIRE TOOLBOX."

It doesn't matter your age either. Money doesn't care how old you are. Money can become a terrible master as soon as you recognize it has the potential to change your status. I know this firsthand.

In middle school, I made hundreds of dollars per week selling drugs, and I spent it as fast as it came in. I got my first bank account at thirteen, and the money gave me a sense of power, prestige, and control. It wasn't even about the money, but about the stuff that the money got me and the attention that came with it. That was its own kind of drug, and I was hooked. I took my friends to the arcade and we blew hundreds of dollars of my money, and it made me a well-liked kid. I had the nicest bike, the best clothes, name brand everything. I kept my parents in the dark by keeping a newspaper route. They thought that is where the money came from, and they didn't pay close enough attention to know otherwise.

Money is not the root of all evil. The *love* of money, though, will take you down. Money is a resource and tool; not the entire toolbox. If you see it as the entire toolbox, you have not only ignored the other powerful tools at your fingertips, but you have given money too much control. The money in your possession is there to be managed well. Harness its power in a way that moves you closer to fulfilling your purpose. How can you execute your purpose well if you are deeply in debt, obsessed with making more, or if you can't pry your own fingers off your funds to give generously?

It took me years to develop a healthy view of money, and one of the most effective ways to get there was by working hard. Generosity came soon after.

YOU KNOW YOU HAVE A PROBLEM WHEN THE POWER GETS SHUT OFF

At fifteen, I did construction work for my brother-in-law. We framed houses and I saved every penny for a car. As my sixteenth birthday neared, my dad told me he would match whatever money I saved, but I had to pay for car insurance and driver's ed. With my saved $250 and my dad's match, a little, gray 1979 Datsun pickup truck was mine.

Eventually, I went to work for a company opening up fast food franchises. I commuted to a location an hour from our house, three days a week after school and all day on Saturdays. At seventeen, I got on a train to Southern California and, just like that, my life as a traveling speaker started. I made $100 a week and it was a simple life. All of my expenses were paid by the organizations I visited. Each week, I gave away $10, put $50 in savings, and lived on $40. I crisscrossed the country for five years, from the Dakotas to Illinois to Michigan, from the east to the west coast. I kept my belongings at home in my garage, and when I married Jami, we lived with her parents. I had very few expenses and I operated entirely in cash.

But things never stay simple, do they? We eventually rented our own apartment, bought a car, a TV and a surround sound system, furniture, and for the first time, we signed up for credit cards to build credit. We still lived within our means. Jami had a job and we weren't nervous about the small amount of debt. Not yet, anyway.

That all changed when we moved to Louisiana. I had a sinking feeling just a couple months into our new life that our finances had flip-flopped. I took a job that planned to pay me $1,200 a month. It was always less than that. We didn't have a savings account and we started putting more on credit cards to make ends meet. I kept hoping the income level would swing in our favor, but it never did. Our spending habits were not in control, but we curbed that quickly as things got more serious. Our utilities were shut off once, and I got scared. We had $10,000 in credit card debt and a car payment, and when our utilities were shut off that one time—I realized we were in over our heads. The stress of it was eating me alive and we declared bankruptcy.

I felt drained. When the power got shut off, my father-in-law stepped in and helped. By that time, we had our first baby and I was ashamed that we had dug ourselves in so deep. I decided to work more to gain some ground, and took a part-time job at a massive retail store that eventually turned full-time. And then our attorney helped me make a decision that would significantly change our lives down the road. He helped us negotiate with the car creditor to keep paying on the car and not include it in the bankruptcy. I had never missed a payment, and it worked in my favor.

While the bankruptcy worked its way through court, I worked and worked at my jobs, consumed by our financial struggles. It robbed me of sleep. It robbed me of peace. I worked two nights a week at the store because it paid better, while still working my day job. Two days a week I stayed up for 24 hours. I did what I do best—work every angle, hustle, and dig my way out.

In July 2005, the bankruptcy was official and we were debt free, except for the car, and that was paid off a year later. Suddenly, I could breathe. I stayed with both jobs, but I stopped working nights and felt incredibly relieved to have no debt hanging over us. We still lived paycheck to paycheck, but with the little bit of freedom we had, we made a new commitment to change our habits. We returned to cash only. No more living above our means. We worked toward four to six months of income in our savings, and we slowly started to build a new financial future.

When I took a job in Victorville, California, we started house hunting, and quickly hit some hurdles. A bankruptcy stays on your record for ten years. It was 2008, right on the cusp of the housing crisis in America. Our banker was stunned to see that our credit score was so high, given our history. He was puzzled until he saw something noted in our file—that car payment we were able to shield from the bankruptcy. We had also filed the bankruptcy only in my name, not Jami's, which helped her maintain a perfect credit history.

Those two things saved our credit score, and without them, we would not have been able to buy our first house in August of 2008. One month later, the housing market crashed. When we sold the house in 2018, we walked away with enough in profit that we transferred it over into a triplex we bought as an investment. The tide had turned—but only because of some unwittingly wise financial moves.

If you're off track, how do you get back on track? It doesn't have to take bankruptcy or sheer luck (like it did for us). It just takes reprioritizing. It takes baby steps—consistently saying no to what the world might say is important in the moment, being able to look ahead to the future you want. It takes saying yes to commitments that will hold you accountable. My wife and I have a rule that we don't spend more than $50 without checking in with each other first. It keeps us both from impulse shopping, and it's like a rubber band, continually pulling us back to each other and the budget we agreed on.

MAKE THE MONEY WORK

Francis Bacon said "Money is a great servant, but a bad master." Those words have echoed in my ear for years. And as I pursued my purpose more passionately, I desired more and more freedom from the constraints finances had on my life. Money is there to serve your purpose. You are the leader. It is not the leader of your life, but so often—by circumstance or decision-making—that gets flipped.

The tragedy is how many people give up, and forfeit the life they could be leading, because they are shackled by debt. You are the leader of fulfilling your purpose, not the resources you have (or lack). Your resources shouldn't govern you. Our bankruptcy awakened us to the idea that our money was like our employee, not the boss.

I have dreams, but I keep myself in check now. For example, I would like to own ten doors someday, meaning enough investment properties that I could count ten front doors with my name on the deed. It's a great dream, and I'm on my way, but we're not going to overextend ourselves. I have bigger dreams than what I have in my wallet right now, and I am aware that building a portfolio is slow and requires purpose.

Your endgame should be a position where you rule, because it's tied to your purpose. You don't ever want your purpose to be limited by your resources. There were times when we almost walked away from our purpose because we couldn't afford to live our purpose anymore. I allowed myself to be robbed of opportunity because I was consumed by debt and the control that money had over me.

I am not a man of regret. I am a man of owning up to your mistakes and then doing it better next time. Our financial lessons were so difficult because they touched every area of our lives—our marriage, our health, our spiritual walks. I wasn't pouring into my family when we were overwhelmed by debt, and that makes my heart hurt.

I COMMITTED TO

REBELLING AGAINST

THE CONTROL OF MONEY

BY BEING GENEROUS."

When you have control of your finances—whether it means you have enough to pay each of your bills or enough to pay the bills of your entire city block—you become free to pursue your passion and the life you were meant to lead with a clear head, healthier relationships, and no guilt. If money has a hold on you in an unhealthy way, you will never fully be able to spread your wings. You can't because you're tied down. I didn't want to be tied down to something that shouldn't have had a hold on me in the first place, and so I committed to being a man of self-control, and that meant sticking to new tenants and then sharing them with others.

The first was to make more than I spent. Yep, sounds obvious, and it is. But you'd be surprised at how many people don't do this (I used to be one, of course.) It's simple math. It's like burning more calories than you consume to lose weight. There's no secret formula. Intake is greater than outtake.

I committed to saving. And if I could rewind the clock, I would have done it earlier. I didn't start my retirement accounts until I was 29, and I felt way behind the curve. If you're 21 and not making a whole lot: yes, open up a Roth IRA with $50 and get started. Make saving a monthly bill you pay.

I committed to rebelling against the control of money by being generous. The best antidote to that poison contaminating your life is to give it away when you can. It doesn't have a hold on you if you don't value it above everything else. Financial generosity not only gives you freedom; it's the cheapest way to be generous.

And decades ago, I had decided I wanted to be known as a generous person.

I have learned to replace that high I used to get from hustling and buying with the consistent, faithful pouring and investing into other people with our finances. Money, it seems, has taken on a whole new life for us, and the best thing about it is that we pull the strings this time.

Let me ask you this, how often during the day do you think about money? If you haven't been a good steward with what you have, and you're reaping the consequences, it is never too late to change the course of your finances. Sit down with your spouse, a financial advisor, someone who will hold you accountable, and make a plan. If your dreams, and your vision, have hit a plateau because you can't afford to pursue the next step toward your purpose, it's time for a change.

UNCHARTED
TERRITORY

Kīlauea is the southernmost volcano on the island of Hawai'i, and weeks before its explosion during the summer of 2018, Jami and I took a day off during a leadership conference I was teaching to hike across its molten crust. It was dangerous and beautiful—the kind of heart-racing, once-in-a-lifetime activity you talk about for years.

To get there, we biked three miles across an expanse of cooled lava fields, the crispy rock crunching beneath our tires. A light rain and wind pushed against us as we crawled off the seats and took off on foot. The landscape deceived us. It looked inviting, like acres and acres of charred, gooey marshmallows had oozed down from the hillside and now stood frozen in time.

In truth, it was dangerous. There was no official trail to follow, and we hopped and hiked across a crust floating atop molten magma. There is always the danger of falling into a hotspot, or more commonly, tripping on the razor-sharp volcanic stone and gashing yourself. We climbed crags and leapt across cracks toward the red-hot glow of lava. We embraced the danger and the unknown, masked by the adrenaline coursing through our veins. And then we felt the heat—not intense at first, but a steady warmth that makes your body sweat and your hands sticky, the rubber of your tennis shoes soften. On broil, an oven can heat to 525 degrees. The average basaltic lava flow is four to five times hotter than that—a toasty 2,000 degrees.

We moved slowly, edging closer as the sun slid beneath the horizon. By the time we laid our eyes on the lava flow itself, we were stunned by its heat and its beauty, once born in the belly of the earth and now rolling across the land like thick cake batter. It could have melted my face, my skin, my bones in minutes. And yet, I stood in awe, not fear. A sense of accomplishment, and contentment, washed over me. What if we had taken a stroll on the beach instead?

To the amusement of the crowd, I threw a walking stick into the lava and watched it burst into flames. It was magical. On the hike back, my mind spun, the parallels between life and the raw power of nature we had just witnessed materialized in my head. Jami and I had just gotten healthy. And not the lose-weight-and-gain-it-back healthy—but the kind of health born from a desire to live longer, adventure further, and honor God with our bodies, minds, and spirits. We lost weight, yes. But, more so, we refocused to live better. Our health journey was a bit like our hike to the lava, and much like many of the journeys we endure in this

PURSUING HEALTH

IN EVERY AREA MEANS

YOU CAN FULLY LIVE

THE ADVENTURE OF LIFE."

life—it starts with hope. It starts off strong, with a fresh perspective and excitement about the newness of it all.

Then, somewhere after the fifth lava tube, the journey gets ugly. You sweat, you get hungry, you question whether to take a right or a left. You leap over a crusty crevice and fall. Bruised and bleeding, you're not sure if the light at the end is strong enough to continue. But it is. It always is.

Pursuing health in every area means you can fully live the adventure of life. It's deeper than self-care, though that is an important element. It's about empowering yourself to accomplish your purpose. If you are not physically, mentally, and emotionally up to the task, you can't do it. And what once was the dream now becomes torture, all because you haven't cared for yourself enough to accomplish it.

TAKING THE DIVE

You might have gathered from the dancing-across-volcanos thing, but I like adventure. My childhood might have imprinted some negatives in my life, but it did one really great thing—it gave me a spirit of independence and boldness. Unfortunately, I haven't always been physically able to take on the adventures my heart desires. In my younger years, I didn't exercise the kind of self-control with food that would lead to health. In adulthood, bankruptcy led me to the kind of stress-eating that packed on thirty pounds in a year.

By the time we pulled up out of our financial mess, I was a mess in every other area of my life. I felt a bit like I was juggling plates. I couldn't keep everything up in the air at once; something had to give. And in that season, it was my health.

Jami and I eventually decided it was time to shed the weight on our bodies that was hindering us from the lives we were meant to lead. We signed up for a program that included a health coach, an eating plan, and a like-minded community.

Within seven months, we lost a combined 140 pounds. We lost an entire person. That astounds me, but something else took place inside both of us that had nothing to do with numbers on a scale. We were free to pursue our purpose with healthy minds and bodies.

I celebrated the results of my health journey by jumping out of an airplane. Because it was something I could not have done a year earlier, there was victory and freedom in this accomplishment.

Jami and I didn't kick off our healthy journeys alone. We had each other, and we had an incredible community cheering us on. It started out as accountability, and what I didn't anticipate was the joy, the laughter, the storytelling of doing this in fellowship with others. The beautiful side effect of letting people in was that I now had a rock-solid community to share in the experience with me. It has made everything so much more profound. These experiences have so much added value and purpose when you are part of a community.

FIND YOUR COMMUNITY

My health journey had awakened something in me—that life is to be shared. It meant a shift in my purpose, to not only help people discover their purpose, but to awaken the possibilities in their life experiences. Alaska was the perfect place to apply that.

I booked a series of talks in a few Alaskan cities, and this time I brought my wife and two girls. I wanted to be very intentional about having shared experiences with my kids and to awaken possibilities in them. What better way to do that than hiking to an active glacier?

That's how we found ourselves climbing across the clear, blue ice of the Matanuska Glacier. Glaciers shift just inches a day, but their size and the strength of the ice slowly carves valleys in the sides of mountains. We hiked slowly, making sure to avoid snow bridges that hide crevasses, sucking in the cold air and laughing along the way. All of a sudden, the glacier emitted a noise that echoed across the expanse and vibrated underneath our feet. We held our breaths, hearts beating faster in our chests. I envisioned the earth opening up and swallowing us whole. Then it was quiet again. I was immediately struck by the frailty of our time here on Earth and how badly I wanted more moments like this with these people.

Our time in Alaska was thrilling and beautiful, and it wouldn't have been possible without living in this new place of health. The energy, the mobility, the perseverance to climb up and all over a glacier with my family would not have been possible with all that extra weight.

Later on the trip, we hiked to two waterfalls and then took a nature cruise through the Kenai Fjords. It was as if we stepped into a National Geographic magazine. Giant pillar arches were overgrown with vines and moss. Bald eagles hovered above the water and then circled back to the coast. A brown bear pawed at a bush and munched on berries. My girls were wide-eyed and enthralled.

I could have done the Alaska tours while I was unhealthy, but I wouldn't have been awakened to the possibilities. I wouldn't have felt ready to do the next difficult thing because I wouldn't have been as willing to take risks, to have the confidence to do the hard hike, to know my footing was sure. I would have been exhausted and nervous, and I wouldn't have been able to enjoy what and who was around me. Health is an invitation to do more, to go further. It takes you places you never would have gone.

When I was unhealthy, I would look around and see unhealthy people around me, of course, but I didn't know the root of their pain, their addictions, their insecurities. Once you link arms with people in a health journey, the blinders get removed. You are not alone. A health journey is an invitation to stare down your fears and find your voice so you can conquer and walk through difficult things. Who can you bring with you? How can you surround yourself with a community?

Hiking glaciers, visiting volcanoes, or whatever is on your bucket list is not about conquering a checklist. If it's not an experience with meaning and purpose, with those that you care about, it won't have as strong of an impact on your life.

HALF DOME

Skydiving, the lava flow hike, and exploring the glacier each lit a fire under me to pursue more, to push harder. I wanted to be more intentional, and that was at the heart of my expedition to hike Half Dome in Yosemite National Park.

Half Dome is a granite mountain peak in the Sierra Nevada mountain range that rises 5,000 feet above Yosemite Valley and soars 8,800 feet above sea level. It's a 15-mile round-trip hike, and it took my hiking group twelve hours to complete. Most of the hike is a challenging climb of switchbacks, and one of the first obstacles is Vernal Fall, a waterfall fed by glacier runoff. We got soaked, but kept climbing until we came to a lake. It was our last place to collect water. We filtered it, filled our CamelBaks, and rested before embarking on more switchbacks.

When we started climbing again, my heart rate did the same. I kept pace with our group, but paused to sit when I knew I needed rest. When we reached the end of the dirt trail, we faced the steep granite slab that would take us straight to the summit. There was no shelter from the elements from this point on, and the danger level increased. Only hikers with a permit, earned through a lottery each year, are allowed past this point.

As we got to the park ranger who checked the permits, one of our group members decided he couldn't continue on. I could easily have been next, but I dug my heels in and rebelled against the voice in my head that told me to quit. Part of that voice was real fear. People have died on Half Dome—nine in fact.

It was a mental game. I was healthier, lighter, more physically fit than I had ever been, but everything inside me wanted to quit. Instead, I pushed that fear down, checked in with the ranger, and set off with my friends.

The granite of Half Dome is not smooth and friendly like a beautiful kitchen countertop. It's jagged and unforgiving. Cables have been hammered into the side of the peak with a waist-high rope. In addition to the cables, there are planks every ten feet up the slope to provide additional footing. You're pulling yourself up a rock wall, beating back fear and burning muscles. My arms grew tired and tingly, my body heavy from the weight of my backpack, and my heart raced the entire climb. I didn't worry about anyone around me. It was one foot in front of the other.

This part of the hike was so much like my health journey. Stick to the system. Stick to the habits. There is something whole and amazing at the end. You set your own pace and you compete only against yourself.

When I reached the top, I knew why I had done it. I stepped onto a platform offering a panoramic view of Yosemite National Park and my breath caught in my throat. I stood on top of the world and tried not to cry. I joined the rest of my group for pictures and sandwiches. We laid on our backs and felt the sun on our faces. As I sat on top of that mountain, I gave myself permission to be proud of my accomplishment. I was up there, staring across the landscape, only because I stuck to my health system and didn't quit. I didn't let failures and obstacles derail me.

The only thing that would have made it any sweeter would have been having more people I loved resting on that granite boulder with me.

The thing about journeys is that they are deeper and more meaningful when you go on them alongside people you care about. I loved that group of guys I was with, but I wished Jami had been there with me. Those feelings got me thinking about who else I could help get to a mountaintop experience. Who else can I bring on my next adventure? Whose hurdles could I help overcome so they can embrace life to the fullest?

As I'm writing this book, we are rallying a small group of people to take on a hiking expedition on the ice sheet of Antarctica. Not a lot of people hike the ice sheets of Antarctica, and it's not something I take lightly. It's going to take some hard work, and it's going to take money and planning. In every map we study, every phone call we make, there's a building of anticipation and expectation of what it's going to take to get there. It will be an eclectic group of people who I have longed to share a life changing experience with. No matter where life takes us after this experience, we will always have this connection.

All of this adventure and connection was awakened by making the choice to lead myself through my health.

UNCHARTERED TERRITORY

When Jami and I had finally peeled ourselves away from that volcano in Hawai'i, we headed back to our bikes in the dark. The air had cooled just enough to be comfortable and the moon lit the path, shining off the hardened lava. As we walked, we slowly realized how amazing this experience had been because our lives had changed so much. We talked the entire way down, and it is something I will never forget. We weren't winded. We had stamina and endurance.

As we talked about this new reality, it kicked off a deeper reflection of our journey. How did we get here? This freedom stirred something inside both of us. If you can get healthy, what else can you do? What other hard thing can you conquer? And more importantly, what else could we awaken in others? Right there in the middle of Hawai'i, we began to dream.

We hiked an unlit, uncharted path that night, much like the new purpose that was unfolding in our lives. Just as you work to get your body healthy to pave the way for new possibilities, your purpose can be awakened when these new possibilities present themselves to you.

For the first time, Jami and I simply asked ourselves who we wanted to be at the end of this life. We didn't answer that question based on the pressure of somebody else's expectations. We didn't use our current talents and knowledge as a limiting factor. Anything we needed to know could still be learned. We just asked, "What's our purpose?" And then finally decided to build the lives we were meant to lead.

WHAT LIFE WILL YOU BUILD?

So let me turn the question to you: What life are you meant to lead? The answer determines what optimal health will look like for you. For Jami and I, it started with a number on the scale because being overweight kept us from the adventures we dreamed about. Our bodies couldn't do what we needed them to do—so that's where we started.

For you, it might mean getting fit enough to race in a triathlon. It might mean better nutrition so you can get rid of brain fog and supercharge your energy. It might mean finally throwing out your cigarettes. Whatever *health* means for you, my hope is that you start. Take the first steps toward a healthier you, so you can show up as your best self. Tackling your life's purpose takes work, energy, and stamina—but there is no better way to live.

TACKLING YOUR LIFE'S

PURPOSE TAKES WORK,

ENERGY, AND STAMINA—

BUT THERE IS NO BETTER

WAY TO LIVE."

Through our health journey, we've learned a few things I think can help you too. In fact, my wife Jami has gotten so passionate, she's helped thousands of people find the same mental, emotional, and physical health we have by becoming a health coach.[2] There are three action steps I'll leave you with.

One: **Plug into a healthy community.** As they say, you become the average of the five people you spend the most time with. So who are you hanging around? Make sure to invest your time with people who are headed the same direction in their health as you are.

Two: **Awaken your inner dreamer.** Take steps to awaken the dreamer within yourself. Imagine being optimally healthy. What would you do that you aren't doing now? How would your life change? What more could you accomplish? Tap into new possibilities for yourself. These dreams can become reality—I promise.

Three: **Find your why.** Your *why* is the foundational reason you truly want something. And it's the most enduring driver of change there is. Health is a journey that gets hard; especially in the culture we live in that's swimming in fast food, sleepless nights, and sedentary lifestyles. When things get tough, you can find the power you need

---

[2] Because you're amazing and obviously the kind of person who wants to grow, Jami has set aside time in her schedule to offer a free health assessment session exclusively for you. Just scan this QR code to pick a time.

to stay the course by remembering your *why*. Deep down, why do you want to be healthy? Is it to be around to play with your grandkids? Or to pass on healthy habits to your own children? Whatever your *why*, live it out and lead by example.

Being healthy doesn't mean having a body that's ready for a movie set in Hollywood. It's about showing up every day as the best mental, emotional, and physical version of yourself possible. I'm grateful for the community we plugged in with to help us achieve our health goals. And I hope these stories and action steps inspire you to pursue optimal health for yourself. Your life has a big purpose—so show up with everything you've got.

LET GO
OF THE DRAGON

In third grade, my teacher called one night to inform my parents I was difficult to manage in class. It was late, so I had already gone to bed, and it was my dad who took the call. I was still asleep when he hung up the phone, came into my room, and pulled me out of bed. He started beating me, hitting me all across my body. His rough hands landed blow after furious blow, and left me covered in bruises. I balled up in the fetal position, confused and shaken when it dawned on me—I had been bad in school and my dad beat me for it. Because there was always one thing that was never tolerated in our house: jeopardizing education.

The rest of the year, I was scared straight. But by the start of summer, I hit a growth spurt, sprinting toward puberty and imagining I was more man than boy. Something in my body and mind said I could do what I wanted.

It was earlier in the school year when my fourth grade teacher called my house one afternoon. By the time I got home, my father was waiting for me. I knew what was coming, and this time when he came at me with his belt, I defended myself.

I pushed back and dodged blows, and when it wasn't as easy for him to find his target, he grew angrier. I felt the tension in the air thicken as if someone was sucking the oxygen out of my bedroom, and in the crescendo of anger and adrenaline, my father lost control, striking my face with his hands and whipping his belt against my legs and arms. There was no aim. He just beat me.

I didn't feel anything in that room. I felt numb. Later that night, I nursed physical wounds that ached and throbbed, but more so anger and sadness that welled up in my heart and spirit. It wouldn't be like this forever, I told myself. One day I'm going to be big enough to not let this happen again.

I recognize what happened that day now, like the slow, brittle freeze of a lake. It was the day my heart hardened. Anger did something strange in me, however. Instead of making me fiery and temperamental—it made me cold and calculating. And over time, my anger solidified into bitter hatred and unforgiveness toward my father.

PLAYING THE GAME

Discipline at my house was inconsistent at best, with the exception of one thing—you didn't screw around with your education.

Education was the ticket out. The non-negotiable. If you messed around with your education, you were punished. The other side of that rule was the understanding that if you did well in school, you could get away with anything else because you had that to fall back on. I knew the game, and I got straight As. I also got the attention of the teachers for messing around, which led to phone calls home, more fights, and more violence.

My parents took school so seriously that we had to be vomiting to miss a day of school. And so the morning after my father had lost his control while beating me, I headed to school bruised and battered. People quickly noticed and it wasn't long before I was in the principal's office, a place I knew well.

I deflected her questions as long as I could until I finally started to piece together my night for her. I cried when I finally told her what happened and felt a bit of weight release from my shoulders. I had told the truth. I released it. I thought it was over. And in my mind, it was time to move on. I was naive. How could I have known what was coming next?

At home, I waited in the living room, staring outside a giant windowpane when I spotted an unmarked car and two police vehicles pulled up at our house. My stomach lurched. My sister answered the door and I stayed frozen to the chair, paralyzed with fear. By the time my parents came home, I was escorted to my room and told to pack a bag. They put me in a police car and took me straight to the hospital, where they had me retell the story.

The doctor measured and photographed each bruise, each mark, noting them on the drawing of a body on his clipboard. I concentrated on the walls of the room, white and sterile.

Many of the beatings happened on my backside, so I was asked to take off my clothes. I stood there exposed, scared, and cold, shame and anger rising up in my throat. But I didn't speak and I didn't cry, instead focusing on a deeper, fresh anger toward my father.

This was his fault.

When I was dressed again, a social worker drove me to Mary Graham Children's Shelter in French Camp, California; a step down from juvenile hall, but a step up from a group home. The jail-like structure meant I was told when to wake up, when to go to bed, when to eat. I missed school for a week and was required to meet with a counselor. After several conversations, she decided it wasn't safe for me to go home and asked if I could stay with relatives. It told her that wasn't an option and she suggested foster care.

During one of our final counseling sessions, she took me to a park. The sun was shining, and we sat across from each other at a brown picnic table. My mind spun at the idea of living with someone other than my family forever. I felt unsteady, like there had been an earthquake in my life and I was scared to walk, waiting for the aftershock.

As we sat there, I asked her what would happen if I went back home and my father hit me again. Her answer stirred something in me. She told me my father could not hit me again or he would go to jail. At that moment I knew I would return home and I would seek revenge. I would aggravate my father until he hit me, and he would be carted off to jail to suffer. I didn't have to wait until I was bigger than him to seek revenge. The power had already shifted.

DESTRUCTIVE BEHAVIOR

My parents came to Mary Graham Hall and we sat through a couple of group therapy sessions before I was released back to their care. When we returned home, it seemed the storm had settled. I returned to school. I met with counselors, and so did my parents, all of us groping in the dark for a new normal. But by the end of fourth grade, I started testing wills again, both in class and at home. My attitude toward my father was very clear— you're not the boss of me anymore.

I refused to listen to his discipline. One day, after he told me not to leave and I had jumped on my bike anyway, he had enough. He chased me down, threw me in the car, and dragged me in the house while I yelled and threatened to call our social worker. Inside, I was hollow and scared, but I covered it with a bad boy façade that rebelled against every authority.

My parents threatened all sorts of punishments if I didn't fall in line with our loosely written house rules. My social worker was called and when all was said and done, there were no

THE MORE I TRIED

TO CUT MYSELF FREE FROM

MY FATHER, THE MORE

HE HAUNTED MY THOUGHTS."

consequences for me. My parents had been bluffing, and I called their bluff.

By the time I was thirteen, I exercised a new, more aggressive bravado. I towed the line with my father at every turn, knowing the power I held over his head. You hit me, you go to jail.

I had to outdo my father. His destructive behavior was my example and I had one goal: to prove to my father that I was better than him. I didn't need my old man, and whatever dirty thing he had done, I could outdo him. Sex, drugs, drinking—I could do it better, faster, further.

The more I tried to cut myself free from my father, the more he haunted my thoughts. I felt bound to him. I could never outdo him, never be satisfied. There wasn't enough sex, enough drugs, enough alcohol to silence the relentless drive to be free of him. The only way to be free was to get rid of him. I could only live the life I deserved if my father was dead.

THE PLOT

I made real plans to kill my dad with a $45 nine-millimeter gun I scheduled to buy from my San Francisco drug supplier. I would buy the gun, wait until everyone was asleep, enter my father's room, and end his life.

Like an actor, I rehearsed the scene over and over in my mind until it was etched into my memory. I wasn't seething with rage, I was cold with my obsession for revenge. It was less about killing him, and more about releasing myself. I thought his death would free me from my pain.

I longed to take ownership of my life, which had spiraled out of control, and yet there was a boulder in the way. Every failure, every pain I experienced, hinged on my father. The weight was too much to carry and I was suffocating. The boulder was never going to budge unless I pushed it off the cliff.

I felt robbed, empty. I got a raw deal, and the way my life was unfolding was not my fault. I wasn't sure why I was even here anymore. I was fourteen years old, mapping out a plan to do to my father what he had done to me the night he beat me. He came into my room that night and robbed me of the life I deserved—and I would rob him as well.

THE TALKS THAT CHANGED EVERYTHING

As intense as my anger was, I encountered something even more powerful just five days before I planned to kill my dad. We'll talk more about it in a couple of chapters, but I'll give away the ending: Because of this encounter, I never bought the gun from my dealer, and never pulled the trigger on my dad. This is profound because I'd already pulled the trigger in my heart. However, my anger didn't magically evaporate just because I didn't carry out my murderous plan.

Over the next few years after this encounter, my rage stayed locked away inside me, keeping an icy grip on my heart. Then, one night I was asked to give a talk at a youth group I'd started attending. The topic? The family of God. Sheesh! How was I supposed to talk about God's family when my own was so screwed up? But I desperately wanted to do well that night, and I dreaded the thought of something going wrong because of my baggage.

Standing in the kitchen, debating myself, I knew what I had to do. I made the decision, then headed to the garage with my stomach in knots. My dad was tucked under the car when I asked him if we could talk. He crawled out and stood, then leaned against the hood. I leaned against the car to match him, then dove into the most nerve-racking confession of my life.

My dad knew a bit about my rebellion, my drug use, the fights. What he didn't know was my heart and my motives, and I confessed it all to him. I had blamed him all these years. I had been trapped in a cycle, and whenever something went wrong in my life, I blamed him. I kept talking, and he listened, somberly, quietly.

And then I got to the gun. I told him about the nine millimeter, the bullets that had been marked for him. At that, his eyes widened, my story sinking in slow and steady.

I told him, "You were five days away from dying, Dad. Five days away from being murdered by me."

The words felt like rocks in my mouth. Heavy and hard to swallow.

I told him the only reason it didn't happen was because I had an encounter with God late one night, alone in my room. I told him because of that encounter, I forgave him for everything. I told him I was sorry for everything I put our family through. I told him I loved him, and I meant it.

He didn't say anything for a few minutes. I remained silent. My father's next words were thoughtful, purposeful, and had locked in place inside me like a missing puzzle piece.

"I never knew," he said.

My mind was blown. How could I have been so consumed with anger and rage at my dad for years, while he was oblivious the whole time?! He'd been days away from getting *shot and killed* by his own son, and he had no idea. In that instant, I realized the only weapon that was used was actually my unforgiveness, and like a smoking gun, I saw that it had only wounded me.

ANOTHER PERSPECTIVE

It was as if I had been living in a house my whole life with one of the rooms locked. I never knew what was inside and, frankly,

I didn't care. Standing in the garage that day with my father shifted my perspective. A door unlocked and I stepped inside.

He had no idea I felt the way I did, and the simple realization of that was freeing. As we talked, I learned about his childhood. He had been abused and tragically mistreated. All he wanted was for us kids to get a good education so we could have a better life than he did. I had never even considered that's why he disciplined me the way he did. So when anything threatened our performance in school, it was like a grenade blowing up in his head. He saw shrapnel exploding into our futures, destroying our prospects. His childhood manifested itself as some poor parenting decisions. He never should have beaten me, but he didn't know how else to do it.

My grandpa (his father) was kicked out of the house by my grandma because he had been a raging alcoholic. My dad was the oldest of three and would go down to the bars to collect as much spare change and child support as he could, just to buy some food for his siblings. His father would spend it all on alcohol.

My dad never had any respect for his own father, and no relationship with him. And in many ways, he became the caretaker of his siblings at a young age. My grandmother worked three jobs as a single parent and eventually remarried another abusive alcoholic. They had three more kids, and my dad's new stepfather was as abusive and destructive as his own father.

So, my dad came into fatherhood with a warped sense of family. He experienced the destruction of his family not once, but twice. Neither his father nor stepfather cared about guidance, or making sure their kids had a roof over their heads and full stomachs, and I could only imagine how that shaped his life.

My whole life, my dad was a workaholic. He grew up around drunk, lazy men, and he didn't want to end up like him. He was damaged, but he loved me. I didn't have the grace to know that growing up. I had never considered there was a perspective other than mine. My brain filled in his intentions. My brain filled in his motives. I thought he was just being a jerk and taking his anger out on me. I was wrong. I added injury to my pain. I was violated by his behavior and abuse, and then I was violated by my own narrative, a story that wasn't even accurate.

Because of that, I trapped myself in a cycle that was slowly killing me and that almost killed him. The bitterness and anger ruled my life. It owned every decision. It even controlled how much pleasure I got out of things.

He ruled and dictated my life, and he didn't lose one moment of sleep because he never knew. It never once affected a decision, never once ruined his day. He wasn't mulling it over at work. Stewing about it when he drove to the store. And yet, I never could escape it. I was imprisoned and he was oblivious.

And isn't that true of all bitterness and unforgiveness? It shackles us to the person, or to the offense, or to the moment.

And while we think it makes us feel better because of a temporary release of anger, or because it focuses our bitterness at the person who has wronged us, it actually never brings more freedom.

It's a brief moment of relief, and then it binds us more tightly to the person. Oftentimes, this person is never affected by your anger, and it's everyone else who suffers. My friends knew I was angry. My teachers dealt with my anger. My mom and sister knew they couldn't handle me because of my aggression and anger problems. Not my dad.

We stood in the garage, the heaviness of our emotions hanging in the air between us.

"You know I love you," he said.

And I did.

"I never meant to do those things to you," he continued. "I was trying to help you get your life focused. I'm not a religious guy, and I'm not sure what you want from me now."

I didn't want much. We had rounded a corner. Things could be different—not perfect, but better.

"I just want to be your friend," I said.

I just wanted a relationship with my dad, no more, no less than every other father and son. That was the summit, the endgame now. To that, he agreed.

UNTIE THE ROPES

I had spent years avoiding my dad's friends and coworkers. And now, I was running into them everywhere, and they seemed especially glad to see me. While I was hating him, my dad had been talking about me at work and with his friends this whole time. He was proud of me. He bragged about me. And now, even more, since I turned my life around and we had reconciled, he wanted people to know. I was amazed. I was witnessing the softening of someone else's heart.

This moment happened when I was 17, and just a few months later, I moved out of the house to travel around the country speaking, and it was during this time that our relationship blossomed into that friendship I wanted. We called each other on the phone at least once a week and our conversations were rich and deep.

Every once in a while, memories of his abuse came back to me and I would wrestle with my emotions. We never talked about it again, but in my own heart, I had to take my thoughts captive. And I had to forgive again. And again. Bitterness had once infected every area of my life, and I had to intentionally work to keep it from making me sick again. Forgiveness, no matter how

FORGIVENESS, NO MATTER
HOW MANY TIMES YOU DO IT,
STOPS THE FLOW OF
BITTERNESS AT ITS ROOT."

many times you do it, stops the flow of bitterness at its root. Eventually, it will dry up and you will be fully free of it.

Today, I am free. I have zero regrets and zero ties to that hard part of my heart. The shackles didn't come off overnight. It's never a one-and-done process. If you have been deeply wounded by someone, one hug, one conversation, one letter will not magically make everything right.

But each of those things can be the first hard step to recalibrating your mind and thoughts toward that person, to forgiving and letting go of the offense and the pain that comes along with it. And with that comes a serious freedom. Never be intimidated to take the step to forgive someone. You might feel overwhelmed by the thought of releasing your pain and anger, but that first step starts the unraveling. And then it's one day at a time. It's like holding a ball of knots in your hand. You untie one knot. And then another, and one day, you will be holding just the ropes, free of knots.

Before I hiked Half Dome, a screw in my leg (from a previous injury and resulting surgery) started surfacing because of my weight loss and had to be removed. Forgiveness is a lot like recovering from a wound. There are phases, chapters, seasons to healing. The first to heal is the surface, the cuts from the surgery. Everything below the surface takes longer, the muscles and tendons and even bone. The superficial cut has to heal first, but what takes the most work to heal is the structural integrity that enables you to walk and move well again.

Even after I started walking again, there was still healing to be done to increase my flexibility. It was necessary, painful hard work to make me whole again. And that's really the difference between a wound and a scar. A wound is still in the healing process. As long as we continue to be led by our emotions, we stay wounded. It could stay an unhealed wound for five years, twenty years, a lifetime. When something touches that wound, we have an oversized reaction because we have left it open and vulnerable.

I have lots of scars. You have lots of scars. And that's a good thing, because it means a wound has healed. You would be amazed at what scars have the ability to do in our lives. They are incredible storytellers. The newest scar on my leg is a scar of victory, perseverance, and purposeful life change. It's a scar of health. It's a map of a journey. You point it out and I'm going to tell you how I got from point A to point B.

Scars are proof of healing, both to you and others. Scars are hope dealers. Scars show that you got through something, and you're not the same. They are like fingerprints, unique to every single person. From a paper cut to an amputation, they are proof that whatever you went through did not end you.

You get to choose every reaction you have for the rest of your life. No one else gets to do that. Each scar is a reminder that you chose to react in a way that moved you toward healing, even if it took a journey to do it. And then you can share that journey with others.

SCARS ARE PROOF OF

HEALING, BOTH TO YOU

AND OTHERS."

TELL THE WORLD

I made a career out of telling my story. I pursued my purpose with intentionality, helping people discover their passion and match it with the plan for their lives. And oftentimes, that meant letting go of the past and finding freedom from bitterness and forgiveness. I've been on five continents telling this story, and now I've put it on paper, in the form of the book in your hands.

In 2012, I was asked to speak at a Father's Day event and I pitched my dad an idea. What if we told our story together? We had spent several years developing our relationship, traveling, doing house repairs, and talking excitedly about computer networking together. We were making new memories, building the stepping-stones we never had when I was growing up. He agreed, but he was worried about sharing in front of a crowd. Our story was still unfolding, raw and fresh, and it was emotional for him.

He agreed to share his story, but wanted to do it by video. It was a great idea and I filmed him beforehand so, during the event, he could answer questions while I presented live to the audience and then cut to him on the video. We included lighter moments, like the time I was in diapers on his waterbed. He was making waves and I was giggling. Eventually I hit a wave and it launched me off the bed. He jumped across the bed and grabbed my diaper, which was enough to break my fall. Then my diaper tears and I fall to the ground while he's left holding the diaper. It was a great "dad moment."

I asked him about his favorite memory, deepest regret, and greatest discovery. He recounted the time he watched us learn to first ride our bikes, or our fastest time at a swim meet. I wove our story together and then I asked him what advice he would give to other dads, and that part has stuck with me since.

"Don't leave things unsaid," was his answer. "Make sure you care about the moments. Make sure you capture the moments, and let love be the driving force."

Two years later, I got a phone call from my mom—she was following the ambulance on the way to the hospital. My dad was sick again. He had been in and out of the hospital that year, including a stint where he was in a medically induced coma while his body fought off infection.

We were in the middle of a birthday party for my youngest daughter—bouncy castle, picnic tables, cake, and a crowd. We wrapped the party early and jumped in the car. I had a feeling something was different this time. When I got to the hospital, he was hooked up to machines but awake and coherent. The medication he was on made it difficult for him to talk, so I cracked some jokes about him being lazy and laying around like a bum. He laughed at my jokes and I'm forever grateful for that.

My father had become a follower of Christ a couple of years earlier, to my great joy. He had missed church while he was sick, so I pulled up the Bible on my phone, turned on worship music, and prayed over him. Soon after, the atmosphere in the room changed. His breathing changed, the nurse came in, and I knew my father was gone.

The room filled with noise and the loud beep of alarms and machines. They tried to resuscitate him, crawling on the bed to do chest compressions. By the time my mom got to the room, they were keeping him alive with machines. I wanted them to let him go and my mom struggled, but finally agreed. I was at my father's side, right where I was meant to be, when he graduated into heaven.

THE STORIES IN OUR SCARS

When I share my story and encourage people to pursue their purpose, I ask them to take a good look at their heart. Are there wounds that really should be scars by now? Is it time to start that process? I ask them if they are shackled to an event or a person. You do not have free range of motion when you're chained. It's why we keep prisoners in shackles. They can't run, they can't jump, they aren't free.

You are free. If you're not, you should be. Forgiveness is about freedom for you; it's not about letting someone who hurt you off the hook. Do the work to get freedom for yourself. That's the life you're meant to lead.

And finally, I ask about the stories their scars are telling. Do you have some scars that could be hope dealers? How can

I encourage you to tell your story? Not because of how bad you've had it, or to one-up someone else, but to share how you have been made whole.

The irony of my journey with my father is not lost on me. When I was a teenager, I had planned to be at his bedside when he died in a much different way. The fact that I was at his bedside when he died, as a son who dearly loved his father and was going to miss the guidance and friendship, is remarkable.

I worked through an incredible flood of emotions. At the hospital, my twin sister showed up high and drunk, and when I fell into bed that night, another revelation washed over me: That could have easily been me. I used to medicate my pain and loss that way too. It was then I also learned that this loss could send me in a different direction than my past downward spirals. This great loss could grow into greater gain.

God wanted to turn my wound into a scar, to use my story to help others who don't know how to lead themselves through something like this. To this day, any time I have a moment or a memory that causes me to miss my dad, I lean into our second life together, which was full of healing, amazing experiences, and conversation. We redeemed our time together. We left nothing unsaid.

I miss him tremendously. I can still hear his voice. I see his mannerisms in my face and my hands. There are echoes of him everywhere. But it's not painful. Scars should never be painful.

They should be healed memories, and that's exactly what I have.

WHAT FORGIVENESS MEANS (AND DOESN'T MEAN)

As I encourage you to forgive, you might be wondering where to start. First, I want you to understand that forgiveness is your choice. No one can force you to forgive them or anyone else— you can't even force a genuine apology. But this is empowering because you actually hold the keys to your own cell. With that control comes the responsibility to make the choice to forgive.

You may also be thinking, *Why would I forgive someone for something they did?* Here's the truth. Forgiveness isn't about them, it's about you. It releases you from a life sentence chained to their offense. Unforgiveness makes you cellmates with your pain. It keeps you locked up, shackled, and emotionally stuck. Understand as well that forgiving someone is not saying what happened to you is okay. Forgiveness doesn't excuse damaging behavior. But it is a personal declaration that you will not be bound by their actions any longer.

Through this process, you will find that every relationship actually gets healthier. This is because unforgiveness is a toxin that invades everything. Even though I didn't know it, my bitterness toward my dad infected all of my relationships. But when I forgave him, it began a process of emotional healing that was truly

FORGIVENESS ISN'T
ABOUT THEM, IT'S ABOUT YOU.
IT RELEASES YOU FROM
A LIFE SENTENCE CHAINED
TO THEIR OFFENSE."

transformative. I stopped clinging to the very thing that was killing me inside.

LET GO OF THE DRAGON

In one of my favorite books, *The Voyage of the Dawn Treader*, by C. S. Lewis, he tells the story of a boy named Eustace. To describe him in a phrase, Eustace was *the worst*. He was selfish, narcissistic, childish, and had every other entitled, crappy trait that makes you dislike someone. To cap it off, he was also greedy.

In the story, Eustace and his companions end up on an island where they find a cave filled with gold. Eustace's eyes glow bright with greed and he curls up on the treasure like a dragon. And in his obsession with the bling, he transforms into a dragon himself. At first, he's delighted to be big and strong, wealthy and secure. But soon, he experiences a deep loneliness, because he realizes he's been cut off from humanity.

This was true in my own life. In hanging onto the dragon of anger, bitterness, and unforgiveness, I became the dragon. It transformed me into someone I didn't want to be. But I didn't know how to escape.

Eustace's transformation happened in a crystal clear well:

> It smarted like anything but only for a moment. After that it became perfectly delicious and as soon as

I started swimming and splashing I found that all the pain had gone from my arm. And then I saw why. I'd turned into a boy again…

The process of transformation hurts; but it's worth it. In hanging onto the dragon, I had become the dragon. To fully step into the life I'm meant to lead, I had to let go of my old identity. Eustace was transformed in a well of the purest water imaginable. I was transformed through a simple conversation with my dad. In both cases, we let go of the dragon.

Remember, forgiveness is a choice, not a feeling. It won't be fun and you will probably dread it—but I promise it will change everything. It's also a process, not a moment. I can't tell you how many times I had to forgive my dad. The memories of abuse never went away, but the more I chose to let go of that dragon, the more like my true self I became. And honestly, this process is messy. You have permission to do it your way. What's important is simply that you start today.

What dragon do you need to let go of?

THE PROCESS OF TRANSFORMATION HURTS; BUT IT'S WORTH IT."

AUTHENTIC
SPIRITUALITY

Have you ever seen *The Matrix*? The movie's main character, Neo, meets a group of crazy rebels trying to get him to take some pills. (Resemblance to my childhood is coincidental.) If he takes the blue pill, he'll remain in blissful ignorance about what's *really going on* in the world. But if he takes the red pill, he'll learn the truth—and once seen, cannot be unseen.

Neo pops the red pill and learns about the horrors of reality. Everyone on the planet lives in a machine-simulated dream world called "the Matrix." Their lives are an elaborate fiction, almost like a real-life video game. Their world, work, and relationships are all an illusion. The truth is that they're all unconscious in goo-filled pods, acting as batteries for the machines.

Pretty heavy stuff.

In a sense, that movie is total fiction. Yet in another sense, it hits on at least part of reality. The world certainly isn't an illusion. But what we can see, hear, feel, taste, and touch isn't all there is to life. There is a hidden part of each of us—the spiritual part. And while it's invisible, we can all feel it.

We are spiritual beings on spiritual journeys. There is an imprint on our souls that sends us constantly searching for our Creator. Much like a cell phone trying to find a cell tower in search mode, we constantly send out signals hoping for an answer back. We are all searching. But life is about more than *what* we're searching for; it's about *who* we're searching for. Because the only one who can tell you why you exist is the one who made you.

As I shared, I took action and made plans to kill my father in anger—but that's only part of the picture. In reality, I wanted a relationship with him so badly that I was devastated that he'd beat me, that he'd treat me like that. It felt like the ultimate betrayal.

I realized this when I confronted him in our garage that day, when he asked, "Tom, what do you want from me?"

I replied, "Dad, I just want to be your friend."

As humans, our deepest desire is to know and be known. And my friend, I believe that is the journey we are on together. So the biggest question is: What do we do about that?

LEAD YOUR SPIRITUAL JOURNEY

In my early teens, I just didn't understand spirituality yet. I had a deep void inside of me, a longing that simply wouldn't stay satisfied. So I tried to fill it with drugs, sex, money, and more. I was on a spiritual search with material things, so nothing was resonating with my soul. Along the way, I started going to a Christian youth group. I didn't have any interest in God, but I did have an interest in a girl. She went, so I did too.

Every week, this ridiculously cheerful youth pastor told me the same thing: "Jesus loves you, and has a plan for your life."

I had no idea what that meant. And quite frankly, I didn't care. However, around this time, things in my life were getting worse. No matter how hard I tried to push away the anger, bitterness, loneliness, depression, and pain, it snapped back at me even harder, like it was connected to some invisible rubber band. I didn't blame God for my circumstances because I didn't even believe he existed. In that moment, I was alone, broken, and with the one person I hated most on earth besides my father: myself. I was dangling at the end of my rope, and in a moment of desperation, I reached out.

On my back at two thirty in the morning I prayed for the first time. It went like this: "Jesus, if you're real like that youth pastor says you are, change me. I don't like who I am anymore." And in that instant, I went to sleep.

I woke up the morning after this first spiritual encounter with God as if I had gulped in my first breath of life-saving air. My whole purpose changed, a purpose that I didn't even know existed. I stumbled out of bed, fumbling for my clothes to make it to my paper route on time. It was my cover for drug money. Somehow, I walked the paper route sober that day. I should've still been high.

I knew that something deep inside my soul had shifted. I was scared, and I didn't know what to do next, but I did know I was open to something I wasn't before. My lungs were clear. My mind was clear. I noticed the crisp, cold air that morning. I noticed the bright blue sky. It was like how a person describes the first time they put on a pair of glasses after their eyesight has grown dim over the years. The colors are beautiful, vivid. And this is how I knew I had a new purpose. I was like a snake shedding its old, flaky skin.

All of this wasn't without some growing pains. What else was clear to me that morning was the heaviness of my past. Suddenly, everything I was doing seemed off—unappealing like food you no longer enjoy. My friends at school noticed right away. There was a lightness about me, a softness. I wasn't angry. I couldn't explain it well either. All I knew is that I wasn't alone anymore.

I went to the school resource police officer and told him everything. He was stunned. He had never heard of a junior high school student living the way I was, using and selling drugs, planning a murder, and then willingly confessing it all.

I just wanted to change; I told him I needed help. He offered to come to my house and watch me flush all the drugs down the toilet and then get me enrolled in a drug rehab program. We called my mom and after school, he met my parents at the house. I knelt by the toilet and dumped each bag of drugs into the water and turned the handle.

I called the phone company and changed my number so nobody in my drug circles could reach me anymore. My parents filled out the paperwork for rehab, and I waited upstairs in my room while they finished with the police officer downstairs. Everything was happening so fast.

My older sister came into my room and asked if I was okay. I hated crying, but the significance of the last twenty-four hours suddenly overwhelmed me, and I cried while she sat with me. I wept over my brokenness, my sin, a new feeling of shame.

More than that, I cried because I finally felt hope.

Whatever faith you have right now, know there is a design for your life. God has a purpose for you. He didn't drop us on this earth only to turn and run. God knows just when we need rescuing. And in those early morning hours in January, he took a 14-year-old boy, beaten down, addicted, anxiety-ridden, depleted, starving for attention, love, wholeness—and he rescued me.

That odd encounter changed me to the core. I know it doesn't happen that way for everyone, and that's okay. I wasn't your

I CRIED BECAUSE

I FINALLY FELT HOPE."

classic addict. The chains broke that night in my bed. God took them. I was done. The lever was pulled and my drug habit was shut off. There were no withdrawals, no flashbacks, no desires, no cravings—I was just done.

Still, I agreed to drug rehab. But after three months, I was ready to leave. It wasn't the environment I needed anymore, and I went home. I stopped partying, and the place that now drew me like a magnet was church.

I was in Sunday service on the weekends and attended a Bible study, a small group, and youth group during the week. I read the Bible—and it started sinking in. Around six months into my newfound faith, my youth pastor challenged me to take the next step and preach a sermon at youth group. And so, on a Friday night in front of hundreds of students that had quickly become like family, I got up and started reading what was essentially my first sermon.

Now, if you've never been to church (or if it's been awhile), preaching isn't just about *reading* Bible verses in front of people; you actually *teach* about what the verses mean. However, my idea of preaching that night was picking my favorite three verses, writing them on a yellow notepad (because I was too nervous to thumb through the Bible in front of everyone) and then read them twice. Then, without any commentary I sat down.

But something else happened in the minute and a half I was up in front of everyone. It was the second time in a year God clearly spoke to me, and it happened mid-verse as I stood on that stage. It might have been a bit of a *Matrix* moment, when everything freezes and goes in slow motion. I was reading and God said, "This is what you're going to do with the rest of your life."

I kept reading out loud. I didn't miss a beat. And yet, I heard God so clearly. It was as if my spirit was conversing with God while my brain and body were doing something else. I didn't feel scared when I heard it. He said it in such an authoritative, yet gentle way. My new purpose was clear: preach, teach, share. To use my story not to highlight pain, but to highlight what is possible with God. I had a story of transformation. He wanted me to tell the world.

I said yes.

Over time, though, it became less about my story of transformation, and more about leveraging my pain. My journey through the bitterness with my dad is not an exclusive journey, and I've connected with hundreds of people who have walked through incredible journeys of pain. When I shared with them, I spoke about bitterness and unforgiveness, and how it eats you alive if you don't deal with it.

My purpose became a laser-focused mission to help set people free by sharing my pain. I started traveling the world—from Russia to parts of Africa to the Caribbean—sharing my story with hundreds of thousands of people. I continued to live a clean life, determined not to hijack my purpose for behavior that would knock me off of that mission. It was during this time that I noticed how many young people knew they had a purpose, but were distracted. And this distraction means that for them, the pivotal moves toward living the life they're meant to lead stay hidden and invisible. But what I've learned is sometimes there are rumblings deep beneath the surface that we can feel and need to pay attention to.

TECTONIC SHIFTS

Have you ever heard of tectonic plates? You probably learned about them in seventh grade science class (or in kindergarten if you were homeschooled). They're massive slabs of solid rock that everything rests on. Yes, that means the coffee shop, house, or park you're reading this book in right now sits atop one of these huge plates. Another interesting fact is that they're always moving. The edges where they meet are called fault lines. Bit by bit, they shift, bumping into each other. And when that happens, everything can change.

At 5:12 am on a Wednesday morning in 1906, every building in San Francisco started shaking. Windows shattered. Brick façades crumbled. Streets ripped in two. And, worst of all, fires raged throughout the city for several days, ultimately destroying 80 percent of the city. It's estimated that over 3,000 people died, making it the highest death toll of any natural disaster in California's history.

Isn't that crazy? Our entire world can be affected by rocks miles beneath our feet? That something we can't even see has the power to change everything within sight? Even if you've never been through an earthquake, this reality hits closer to home than you may think.

Confession: I'm not actually that interested in rocks. So why the geology lesson? Because tectonic plates are a lot like the forces below the surface of lives. Deep within us are things that shift, bump, and rumble, changing the landscape of our lives. I'm talking about our spirits.

If you take anything away from this chapter, remember that you're a spiritual being on a spiritual journey. Even though you can't see it, you have a spirit that matters. And just like those crazy big tectonic plates, what happens beneath the surface changes everything we see.

WHAT'S NEXT?

Meeting Jesus was a tectonic experience that changed my life forever. You can honestly call it a transformation. Maybe you already have a relationship with God through Jesus. Maybe you used to, but somewhere it got hijacked by life, and you lost touch. Or maybe this is the first time you've ever heard about how he likes to save 14-year-old drug addicts like me! No matter where you're at, you can take the next step toward spiritual growth.

FAITH ISN'T LIKE A
FAMILY HEIRLOOM THAT
CAN BE PASSED DOWN;
IT'S SOMETHING YOU HAVE
TO OWN FOR YOURSELF."

I have good news for you. Spiritual growth isn't as abstract as we make it out to be. It may seem like there is some magic formula, some secret to the success of a spiritually mature person. But guess what? That couldn't be further from the truth.

We are each invited to grow. And in my experience, there are three steps everyone has to take to authentic spirituality. There are no cuts in line, or any people who have special access to God that you don't get! You simply need to:

- Invest in your soul every day by reading the Bible and praying.

- Engage in a Jesus community: at church and in a small group.

- Activate yourself in service to others.

I named this chapter "Authentic Spirituality" because your faith must become *authentically* yours. Faith isn't like a family heirloom that can be passed down; it's something you have to own for yourself. You can't borrow it from a friend. The Jesus who my youth pastor kept telling me about didn't want a proxy relationship through someone else—he wanted Tommy Hammel. As messed up as I was, Jesus chased me down.

I'm inviting you to own your spiritual journey and start leading yourself to where God is calling you, without a preconceived notion of what that should be for you. You can have a new start right now.

You just have to humble yourself enough to invite him in.

LET'S GO TO SPACE MOUNTAIN

When I met God, I had no idea what was in store. I had no idea that Jesus worked such a massive change in my life. Honestly, it felt like a kid who expected a carousel ride but got Space Mountain instead. So I'm inviting you to the Space Mountain of spiritual experiences. Something that might seem so small and insignificant is actually the most real and most valuable part of you. You are a spiritual being on a spiritual journey. And the only thing that can satisfy you is the Spirit of God himself.

I know this might seem like a lot, but I promise you, it's simpler than you might think. If you're wondering where to begin your new spiritual journey—or just looking for a fresh start—I had some friends put together a free resource with YouVersion. It'll meet you right where you're at and help you understand the Bible in a brand new way. Scan this QR code to begin a daily reading plan that will guide you in the right direction.

WHAT NO ONE
TOLD YOU ABOUT
LEADERSHIP

Early one morning in a small mountain town, I stood in line at the local coffee shop. I smiled at the barista as I ordered my usual coffee.

"How's your day going so far, Brittany?" I asked brightly.

She stopped tapping in the transaction for a second, almost baffled at hearing her name from some random guy in a flannel shirt.

"Uh, good, I guess?" she replied. (It was more a question than a statement.)

I kept talking, thanked her by name once more, and then shuffled down to the end of the bar for my drink. Yep, I'm a "name guy."

It might seem silly, but years ago, I set a resolution to address every single person I could by their name.

Names are powerful things. How do I know? Well, my friend, out of the 171,146 words currently in use in the English language, I know your favorite one without even meeting you. That's because it's mine too. That magic word is your name. Psychologists have found our names are so powerful, hearing them actually influences:[3]

- The kinds of people you like.

- The kinds of foods you like.

- What you do for a living.

- Where you live.

- And many of your major decisions.

As Dale Carnegie once said, "A person's name is, to that person, the sweetest and most important sound in any language."

In this chapter, we're going to talk about leadership. And while using people's names can certainly help you win friends and influence people, there's a different kind of leadership a lot of people skip. A lot of really good leadership books, courses,

---

[3]Tim David, "The Most Important Word You'll Ever Use," Psychology Today, Sussex Publishers, 23 Feb. 2015, www.psychologytoday.com/us/blog/the-magic-human-connection/201502/the-most-important-word-youll-ever-use.

TED talks, and conferences share amazing principles to start movements and lead people to do great things. But they're a bit like trying to leap up a flight of stairs, because they don't start with step one.

That starting place has everything to do with your favorite word. It's about *leading yourself*. Leadership is odd because it's two-pronged. It's about leading yourself before it ever becomes about leading others. And ironically, you are often the hardest person to guide! If you're ever going to find the life you're meant to lead, you need to find a way to get moving in the right direction. During my greatest seasons of growth, I did the hard work of leading myself. Now I invite you to do the same thing—to do this, let me tell you some secrets.

3 SECRETS OF SELF-LEADERSHIP

Remember in school when a friend would start a sentence like this: "Can you keep a secret?" Obviously, whether you'll actually keep it or not, you're going to say, *Yes, of course I can!* Then, you could lean in for the juicy gossip. You usually found out things like Jenny has a crush on Peter, or Eddie cheated on the math test. As kids, these secrets seemed like the kinds of things that could destroy you.

Well, I want to share three secrets with you. But here's the trick, I want you to tell them to everyone. While you're not going to learn who has a crush on whom or who cheated on their math test (also known as *taxes* as we get older), you will learn three ways to lead yourself that few people talk about. Ready? Secret one is about tapping into your genius.

SECRET ONE: PLAY TO YOUR STRENGTHS

Remember Superman? He's got super strength, he can fly, he shoots laser beams from his eyes, and he even can spin the world in reverse to travel back in time. Those are some nifty abilities. But he has one major weakness: *kryptonite*. For some reason, this green glowing rock can make him as weak as a goldfish. When he's around kryptonite, he collapses in a heap of frailty and shame (a.k.a. middle school gym class). Obviously, Superman should do everything in his power to avoid kryptonite, right?

Actually, no. If he hyper-focused on avoiding kryptonite, his energy would be used to run instead of standing and fighting. You and I are both kind of like Superman. We all have natural strengths and weaknesses. But sometimes we focus so much on our weaknesses we forget our strengths. So let's get you back to shooting laser beams out of your eyes.

I am a task-oriented person. I like lists. I'm organized. I've got systems that I love to follow because they're how I get things done. I've got that nailed. What I didn't have locked down was how to take the time to see people where they're at and for who they are. Instead, for years I saw people as a means to get to my objective. And even though my objectives and intentions were good, like feeding people in impoverished countries or helping troubled kids, I approached people like they were a mine. I wanted to get in, find the resources I needed, and then get back to my own work.

Relationships were one of my kryptonites. As a leader, I learned that I couldn't churn and burn through people if I was ever going to build something that lasts. Maybe for some of you, it's the opposite—relationships are your strength and discipline is your weakness. No matter what your superpower and kryptonite combos are, I want you to focus on the bright spot of your strength.

My gut reaction was to throw out my systems so I could be more organic, relational, and nurturing. You know, to avoid my kryptonite. If your weakness is discipline, you may be tempted to throw out your focus on relationships and get more tactical with people. But this is where self-leadership comes in handy. Play to your strengths rather than covering your weaknesses.

Instead of throwing out my systems, I simply made developing real relationships part of my systems. From simple interactions like ordering coffee, looking people in the eyes, and saying their name with a smile, to putting personal check-in time at the top of every meeting agenda. (Yes, I actually write *check-in time* into meeting agendas.) And then I genuinely listen to my colleagues' answers. My systems determine habits, which determine success.

I built my own system, which at first seemed very mechanical. The first was addressing people by their name. Why? Because

THE WORLD DOESN'T NEED YOU TO BE A COPY-PASTE VERSION OF SOMEONE ELSE."

I want to see them. If I get the system to see them, then I'm going to have the habit of seeing them. And that way, I am able to achieve my goal of finding and discovering people's strengths, right? Take a few minutes to reflect:

- What are your strengths?

- What do you love to do more than anything else?

- What are your weaknesses?

- What do you hate to do more than anything else (that still needs to get done)?

- How can you work on your weaknesses by harnessing your strengths?

Answering these questions will be clarifying and motivating because the first secret to leading yourself is operating according to your unique gifts. The world doesn't need you to be a copy-paste version of someone else. It needs you to be the best version of yourself, and that means playing to your strengths—which is also the path to becoming a world-class leader.

SECRET TWO: TAKE THE HUMBLE PATH TO BECOMING WORLD-CLASS

Whether or not you enjoy golf, Tiger Woods is a world-class athlete. And he's absolutely dominated his sport. One day I was thumbing through the channels during the height of his career.

No matter which golfer was on the screen, all the commentators were in a tizzy over Tiger. And for good reason—he's been the number one player in the world for the most weeks of any golfer in history. He has been awarded PGA Player of the Year 11 times—more than any golfer in history. He's front of the pack for all active golfers in career major wins and career PGA Tour wins. He is the youngest pro golfer *ever* to achieve the career Grand Slam—meaning he's won all four of the golfing world's "Super-bowls" in a single calendar year. In fact, Tiger was so proficient that the announcers on TV that day said tournament organizers had tried to "Tiger-proof" the course. That's how much he shaped the entire sport of golf.

I watched Tiger on the screen. He squared up, paused, and swung. The ball was still in midair when the commentator mentioned that Tiger's swing coach had helped him refine his approach to the ball. Wait... what? Tiger Woods has a swing coach? *The* Tiger Woods?

How does the number one guy in his field improve on being *numero uno*? Why does number one even need to be better? Because Tiger Woods' drive wasn't only to be number one. He was in competition with himself. And he's not the only one. We could take a lesson from basketball great LeBron James, who is a three-time NBA champion, four-time NBA MVP, and two-time Olympic gold medalist. Chris Jent coached for the Cleveland Cavaliers from 2006 to 2011, but was essentially LeBron's personal trainer. Who would imagine that LeBron James, arguably

EVEN THE BEST

HAVE COACHES."

one of the most talented basketball players to play, needed pointers? But he did, and he still does. Even the best have coaches.

The great become greater—but not by accident.

I'm not number one in anything in the world. Even in the things I'm good at, I'm not number one. When I look at Tiger and LeBron I realize if they need coaches and mentors speaking into their lives, I need them ten times as much. The adage rings true: Amateurs learn by trial and error, professionals learn from a coach. I don't want to live below my potential, and it means I have to lead myself by inviting input in my life from voices who will help me grow.

Becoming world-class is about giving someone permission to speak into your life—to challenge, correct, and change you. This takes humility. And, in many senses, it means leading yourself by becoming a follower of the right people.

I regularly map out places where I want to be number one in my life. Then, I identify and seek out those who demonstrated the ability to do those things well. It doesn't matter what area needs insight—business, finances, marriage, parenting, speaking—I'm best when I invite wise counsel into my life. This doesn't mean I'm trying to become mini-versions of them. Instead, it means they're bringing out the best in me, refining my strengths, and giving me perspective on my weaknesses. Consider these questions:

- Where do you want to become world-class?

- What areas are you good with right now, but know you can become greater in?

- Who can you invite to speak into your life in these areas?

- Are you prepared to be humble, listen, and learn?

- Are you searching for someone who can help you achieve your purpose faster than you could on your own?

Becoming world-class takes surprising humility. It means leading yourself by following the right advice, instruction, and experts. But guess what? There's another, more difficult layer to humble self-leadership, and it's secret number three.

SECRET THREE: INVITE FEEDBACK FROM SURPRISING SOURCES

Accepting input from expert coaches and seasoned mentors makes sense. If Tiger and LeBron do it, it's hard to argue with. But what if I asked you to invite feedback from people who aren't as skilled as you in your strengths?

As a speaker, I've spent years listening to more experienced speakers. But my effectiveness skyrocketed when I created my first speaking team. This was a diverse group of people who represent the audiences I share with. They have different backgrounds, dreams, gifts, and ambitions. And even though they were "out there" while I was on the stage, I realized I needed their input to lead myself toward growth. Here's why.

I'm a one-dimensional person. I'm a male, a dad, a husband. This means I naturally see things from that perspective only. One day I asked myself, *What if I invited a female perspective on my topics?* After all, half to two thirds of my audience were typically female, but they were only hearing life from a male's perspective. This meant there had to be gaps.

Next, I don't consider myself a very creative person. I'm structured—sometimes to the point of living in the proverbial box. So I built my speaking team with another layer, bringing in creative people for their perspectives. It's a symbiotic relationship. Bringing them along on the journey validated their views and honored them. Secondly, I became a much better presenter, and my content connected with a much wider audience.

I also asked for input on learning styles. I know that I absorb information a certain way, and it's fascinating to me that we all learn differently. Because I kept my own learning style at the forefront of my communication, I risked missing a connection with huge portions of my audience. This meant I was under-serving thousands of people every year. How could I try to meet everyone where they're at? I know I can't perfectly communicate to every single person—but I can get better.

I started to peel back layer after layer as I learned different ways how I could become a better presenter. In the end, I discovered a bunch of blind spots. This process has made me a much more engaging and helpful speaker. Now, let's think about you:

- What is your natural perspective on life?

- What perspectives are you missing?

- Do you value diverse input in your life and work?

- Is it in your heart to serve people well, even if they aren't like you?

- Who can you invite perspective from—not only from "experts," but those who have different points of view than you?

Every day I learn that leadership takes more humility than I thought. It isn't about power or position, it's about serving people to help them reach new heights. To lead others, we must lead ourselves by accepting a diverse array of perspectives, opinions, and critiques. It isn't easy. But nothing worthwhile ever is.

A practical way to start is with a personality assessment. There are a bunch you can take for free that will help you see yourself in a brand new light. You'll gain perspective on your strengths and find areas where you can improve. Best of all, you'll understand yourself better, which means you can lead yourself better.[4]

---

[4]If you want a kickstart on the different personality assessments, where to start, and how to use them, you're in luck. I recorded a podcast episode on this just for you. Just scan the QR code to give it a listen.

YOUR IDENTITY MAP

You don't accidentally meander down the path of self-leadership. It's a trailhead you arrive at and then decide to walk. So where are you meant to go? Who do you want to be? What kind of dent do you want to leave in the universe? To go there, you must lead yourself.

I don't think there's anything truly special about my journey—lots of people have experienced challenging childhoods, lots of people have been redeemed, lots of people have found their community. I just want to use my story to inspire people to make the changes—however hard they may be—to confidently walk toward the future they are made for.

How do I make sure I'm doing that, instead of getting sidetracked by life? Well, you know me, I have it mapped out. I created an identity map, sort of like a GPS for how I want to lead myself in the next twenty years. By the time I turn sixty, I want to be world-class in these four areas: family, finances, health, and mentorship.

FAMILY

First, I want our family to be known as a safe place to dream and fail. I want a legacy of risk takers, failure makers, and learners. I long to create a family culture driven by experiences, not materialistic stuff. This means valuing the experiences of doing hard things together, like hiking glaciers. It means memories of our wild adventures outshine our Christmas and birthday presents. Most importantly, I want to lay a vibrant spiritual foundation for my daughters and their kids… and continuing down our generational line.

FINANCES

In finances, I want to be known for extreme generosity. I want to be financially free so my family can give to the right things. I want money to work for us, not the other way around. I want to be known as the guy with residual income, that we've set up streams that feed future generations' dreams and possibilities. I want to be generous, by seeing other people's potential and providing opportunity for their growth. I want to take the gifts, the opportunities, and give them away as much as reasonably possible. In the end, I want our finances to be a vehicle of blessing for generations to come.

HEALTH

In the area of health, I want to be known as a man who took great care of my body. And not according to a scale, coveted image, or pant size, but because I wanted every ounce of energy possible to fulfill my purpose. Health means the ability to accomplish my goals, the agility to move and serve, to travel and to take on new adventures. I never want health to be a limiting factor, if it's within my control. I want to be around long enough to see the possibilities for my grandkids and beyond.

MENTORSHIP

Finally, I want to be known as a mentor—someone who communicated well and deeply to the people around me through writing, speaking, guiding, and sharing. I want to be known as someone who could connect and relate, and move people to action—to chase their purpose with intentionality. I want to be someone who is known for being present. As a man who mentored not just from the stage or a platform, but in real day-to-day life. Who stood with people in the muck and trudged out alongside them. I want to journey with people.

LIFE IS AN ULTRA-MARATHON

As we've all heard, life is a marathon, not a sprint. But I don't think that goes far enough. Let's up the ante and say, "Life is an ultra-marathon, not a marathon." Okay, that doesn't have the same quippy ring to it. However, I think it's true nonetheless.

Ultra-marathoners often run 100 miles or more. This means running for days at a time. Even though they're running an individual race, and no one else can take their strides for them, they don't go it alone. They have a support team that offers food,

SELF-LEADERSHIP

IS ABOUT HAVING

THE HUMILITY TO INVITE

OTHERS INTO YOUR

JOURNEY."

water, medical care, and healthy doses of encouragement all along the route.

While we have to personally discover our purpose and run toward the life we're meant to lead, this doesn't mean going it alone. We need a support team in life and leadership. To lead ourselves well means finding our support team. It means running alongside people we can trust—coaches, mentors, friends, peers, and diverse voices who have our best interests at heart, because we have their best interests at heart as well.

The three secrets of self-leadership boil down to a single phrase: Don't go it alone. Self-leadership is about having the humility to invite others into your journey. To submit yourself to healthy critique and then actually make adjustments based on those feedback loops. It's easy to read (and even to write), but it's hard to do. However, I believe you can do it. I hope you do too.

Now, let me ask you one last question: Can you keep a secret? I sure hope not.

LEADERS
PASS THE MIC

Do you know why birds sing? They aren't simply saying sweet things to one another or trying to chat with Mary Poppins. Birds sing to mark their territory. They chirp to let other birds know: "Back off, this is my bird feeder and imma lose my mind if you land on my turf."

Seriously, birds are jerks. Just ask my wife Jami, who was pooped on by birds two trips in a row. The first time, we were sitting in our car at the beach and she had her window down just a crack when in drops a bomb, splatting on her leg like a glob of sunscreen. The next time, they upped the ante and went for the headshot. So the birds have clearly marked their territory with Jami (which is why no one stands next to her at the beach anymore).

But they're not the only creatures who mark their territory. Dogs pee on everything to lay claim to their domain. Bears do a weird little dance with saplings and shrubs called *straddle marking*.

And humans wear masks to indicate a border of six feet must be respected. Well, that's kind of a new one.

There's another brand of territorialism I want to talk about though. And while it's pretty natural, it isn't good. I've worked with a diverse array of leaders in my life. Some of them were drug dealers, others were nonprofit leaders. But the most telltale mark of bad leadership is the fear of being overshadowed.

These are the leaders who want to be center stage all the time. Who are paranoid and always on guard, watching their team like a hawk to ensure no one is challenging their authority. This means they're threatened by talented people, instead of excited at the thought of helping them reach their full potential.

Leaders like this might even go so far as to sabotage others. Everyone's heard of the Golden Rule: Do unto others as you would have them do unto you. Well, territorial leaders follow what I call the Fool's Golden Rule: *Do unto others before they do unto you.*

Last chapter, we looked at three secrets to self-leadership. They all orbited the same thing: humility. In this chapter, we're going to look at the other side of the coin, leading others. What you'll find is the same posture of humility is required to be the leader you're meant to be.

Before we go on, I want you to imagine a Broadway musical. You don't have to like them. Just picture the elaborate set design. The actors and actresses decked out in crazy costumes.

The thousands of people packed in the theater to watch. Who are the leaders in this scenario? The director? Sure. The actors? Makes sense. But what if there were leaders everyone forgets about, but who are just as important? What if the real leaders are the technical crew?

Think about it like this: They make the show visible to everyone in the audience. They understand that without the talented actors stepping into the spotlight at just the right moment, or without their mic being set just right to hear their beautiful vocal performances, there is no show. However, without the crew's willingness to shine light on and amplify the voices of their team, all you've got is a bunch of weirdos dancing in the darkness.

So, we're going to consider a different measure of leadership. It isn't about which mics you hold, but the ones you give away.

WHAT IF LEADERSHIP ISN'T WHAT YOU THINK IT IS?

Now, you might be saying, "Tom, I'm not a leader. I don't want to be a leader. Leadership doesn't interest me. In fact, I thought this book was about me and the life I'm meant to lead?!"

Fair enough. But can you consider for a moment that you were made to lead? It might not be from a platform, stage, or screen. Everyone making a positive impact on the world (which your purpose will do) has influence over other people. And I'm with

SOMETIMES LEADERSHIP

IS AS SIMPLE AS GETTING

OUT OF THE WAY."

the leadership guru John Maxwell who put it like this: "Leadership is influence."

Even if you don't consider yourself (or aspire to be) a leader, I want you to stick with me. Because I think leading others is as counterintuitive as leading yourself—it isn't about what most of us think it is. Sometimes leadership is as simple as getting out of the way.

The longer I've been a *leader* in the official sense—in charge of developing hundreds of other leaders and their teams, and managing employees and volunteers—the more I've learned the real trick is to make it other people's turns. When I realized this, things started to get really fun.

Every time I was with someone, I hunted for opportunities to let them shine. In meetings, I tried to highlight others' ideas. I made it a point to publicly celebrate the accomplishments of other people. Instead of trying to build my resume, I found places where I could step out of the way. This absolutely terrifies territorial leaders because they believe they'll lose every shred of credibility and authority they've worked so hard to earn.

My experience tells me the exact opposite. Because right when I let go of my own territorial tendencies, and started clapping for other people, something surprising happened. The more credit I gave away, the more influence, authority, and significance I got back.

To be fair, I don't think it's that territorial leaders always want to be in the spotlight. I think we fear loosening our grip because people might realize they don't need us. If you can do what I'm doing, do you really need me? And worse yet, what if you can do it better than me?! That seems like a recipe for a pink slip.

But what I have proven to my own heart is that hogging the credit and clawing at the limelight to prove my value is the most backward way to lead. The more I gave away to people, and the more opportunities I made for others to have their turn, the more invaluable I became. In fact, this practice still serves me to this day.

People tell me no one gave them an opportunity like I did. And that opportunity played a part in their success. Do you see what's happening? Instead of people pointing at you and asking, "What do I need you for?" they give you a hug and say, "Thank you for giving me the opportunity to grow." Here's the truth. Every time I make leadership about me first, I fail. But when I make it my mission to give the mic to other people, to share the stage, to let others stand on the platform and shine, my leadership value grows exponentially.

Leadership is about helping others find and fulfill their purpose. This is the life we're meant to lead. So, by starving territorialism and finding joy in other people's success, you can become the most influential leader you're capable of becoming.

Now that we've held our humble pep rally, let's talk about the next skill this mic-passing style of leadership requires.

LEADERSHIP IS ABOUT HELPING OTHERS FIND AND FULFILL THEIR PURPOSE."

A TRUE SAFE SPACE

I've spent a lot of time speaking to and leading groups of teenagers. If ever there was a definition for herding cats, that was it. Even so, I loved giving kids the opportunity to shine, grow, and discover who they were made to be. Let me ask you this, have you ever given the mic to a 14-year-old boy who has no clue what he's doing, in front of hundreds of adults, and your boss all at the same time? I have. And let me tell you, this is where the rubber meets the road on my leadership philosophy.

I once let a group of students perform a skit to illustrate a teaching point, and one of the students who was a little rough around the edges used profanity in front of the entire crowd (I'm talking rows of 80-year-old, purple-haired ladies named Mavis.)

I could feel the eyes of the crowd, and the students, snap to me. How should I react? My reaction would set the tone for everyone else's. I deliberately chose not to react in the moment. I let the kids move on and keep going as if nothing happened. When it was all over, I chatted with him. He apologized profusely, obviously embarrassed, and I simply asked him what lessons he learned. I wanted to help him fail successfully and understand that he's held to a higher standard when leading.

You see, if I would've laid into him or been visibly upset in front of everyone, he wouldn't have learned how to do better next time. Instead, he would've learned to make sure there was no next time. I went to our leaders and let them know what happened and how I handled it, and they were all onboard. Slipups are going to happen because people aren't perfect. But a leader's job is not to create perfection—it's to instill confidence that it is safe to grow here—because all growth takes risk.

We also created an atmosphere of celebration at the youth group. Anytime someone took a risk—from little things like making an announcement to singing on stage with sweaty palms—I paused our programming and we celebrated together.

Here's an important distinction though. A leader's job isn't to remove the risks. Instead, it's to create a safe place to land if they fall. It's a lot like bouldering, a sport where climbers crawl up challenging boulders that can be more than twenty feet high. There's a lot of falling. But they climb with thick mats below when they lose their grip or miss a handhold. A leader is a lot like that bouldering mat. It's not about trying to stop your climbers from falling, it's simply being there to support them when and where they do.

I understand people will mess up, and some may be less refined than me. Certain things might lack polish. But my job isn't to create a perfect product—it's to build strong leaders. In my role of empowering people and helping them lead the life they're meant to lead, my job is not to remove the risks, but to remove the anxiety and fear of taking a risk.

I bring the most value by empowering the productive failure loops we talked about in chapter two. And even when someone on the team failed in front of me, or with me, I never punished or chastised. Rather than coming at them with immediate corrections, I came with questions. Learning the lesson was more important than me correcting their behavior. If they truly learned the lesson, they would naturally change their behavior.

EVERYONE NEEDS A WINGMAN

Sometimes all people need to be successful is a wingman or woman. This was never more clear to me than during the last eighteen months of a stint working with a group of teens. During that final stretch, I didn't fully write my own sermons, I didn't design the programming for our events, I didn't even work with people individually during special response times, where students could get help, prayer, and support. And it was one of the greatest stretches of growth of my career.

I had a message-writing team, who helped me craft what I would speak about. I had a team of leaders who organized events from top to bottom, and I had twenty-five students we trained to help their peers during the response time.

I gave that special team this commitment: Show up prepared to help your fellow students, but if someone comes with a situation that's too much for you to handle, look over your shoulder, make eye contact with me, and I'll be there beside you in a few steps. I was their wingman. But do you know what? I never had to go help any one of them. They were more capable than they knew. Best of all, they made a bigger impact on other peoples' lives because I didn't take over for them.

YOUR CALL TO ACTION

The world is waiting for leaders to step up, grab the microphone, and then give it away. Our goal is not to bulldoze our way to the front of the line, but to create opportunities for the people we're leading. So if you love people and want to see those around you thrive, I'm calling you to action.

It's time to rebel against the fears that have paralyzed you. The fears that have held you back from the life you're meant to lead. I want to challenge you to take risks and to understand there are often more lessons in the failures than there is pain. I'm telling you that if you have an influence on even one other person, you are already a leader. The only question is what kind of leader do you want to be?

Be intentional with every acquaintance, coworker, friend, and family member. Some of your relationships will last years, some a few lunches, and others simply for a coffee break. But you can make a positive impact on them all, as a new kind of leader—the kind that lives to shine the spotlight on others. That loves to celebrate the mic drop moments when other people win.

I'M TELLING YOU THAT

IF YOU HAVE AN INFLUENCE

ON EVEN ONE OTHER PERSON,

YOU ARE ALREADY A LEADER."

Here's your call to action:

1. Can you ask questions and be more interested in others than you are in yourself?

2. Can you be on the hunt for ways to help others shine?

3. Can you be a safe place for others to fail?

If you answered yes to any of these questions, then you've already answered the question the beloved poet Mary Oliver asked, "Tell me, what is it you plan to do with your one wild and precious life?"

I hope you're ready to live the life you're meant to lead and to bring others along for the journey. You can't hear it, but I'm clapping for you right now. Onward.

ACKNOWLEDGEMENTS

Thank you to Andrew Guerra, Dave Ross, David Specht, Donovan Ross, James Gravell, and Kylie Hammel. My cultivation crew. Together we are awakening purpose and potential in the world.

To Jordan Loftis and the team at Story Chorus. There is no way I would have walked this journey alone. Thank you for your partnership and pursuit of excellence that makes me look better than I am.

Next, I want to thank some of my countless mentors, including: Jim Reid, Doug Reid, Dale Everett, Sam Farina, Kevin Shorey, John Martin, Dennis Reynolds, among so many others. This book is really your story. What you've poured into me has shaped, molded, challenged, and cheered me on to become the person I am—and hope to be.

Finally, thank you to the three most important and amazing women in my life. Brittan, who now demolishes me at Halo.

Kylie, who has become a more skilled negotiator in arguments than me. Daddy is so proud of both of you. I love watching you become incredible, powerful women as you create the lives you're meant to lead! To my hot wife Jami, my life leadership partner... a million dreams for the world we're gonna make!

ABOUT THE AUTHOR

Tom Hammel has a passion for leadership development and to see people mobilized to their purpose. Having been given the opportunity to speak when he was fifteen, Tom was trained in an environment that believed in seeing young people empowered. Tom has served at churches and organizations of various sizes and currently serves as the Executive Director of Leadership and Church Ministries for SoCal Network. One of his passions is to raise up young leaders and see them discover their calling and purpose. Tom and his wife Jami have been married for 20 years and together have two daughters, Kylie and Brittan.

Connect with Tom:

@ | @tomhammel

f | facebook.com/tom.hammel

https://www.ourcultivatedlives.com/